Titles by Janvier Chouteu-Chando

The Usurper: and Other Stories
Triple Agent, Double Cross
Disciples of Fortune
The Union Moujik
Splendid Comets
Flash of the Sun
Fortune Calls
Fortune's Master
Fortune's Children
The Norilsk Bears
To Be In Love and To Be Wise
The Fire and Ice Legend
The Sweetest Madness
The Grandmothers
The Hunger Fire
The Shades of Fire
Father and Sons
The Doctors
Dark Shades
Fateful Ties
The Verdict of Hades
His Majesty's Trial
Ngoko's Folly
The Usurper
The Dowry
I am Hated
The Oaf

Non-Fiction Titles by Janvier Chouteu-Chando

THE CANARY IN A COAL MINE EFFECT:…Assassinations..
FALLEN HEROES: African Leaders Whose Assassinations…
BROKEN ENGAGEMENT: Why a Donald Trump Win…
THEIR LAST STAND: Donald Trump's Upset Victory…
Ukraine: The Tug-of-war between Russia and the West
Cameroon: The Haunted Heart of Africa

The New Africa

Getting Rid of the Puppets and Dictators,
Dismantling the Anachronistic Political Systems
and Reversing the Retarding Influence of the
Mafia-style Foreign Relationships

Janvier T. Chando

TISI BOOKS

NEW YORK, RALEIGH, LONDON, AMSTERDAM

PUBLISHED BY TISI BOOKS
www.tisibooks.com

EPIGRAPH

"The time for revolutionaries with the complete freedom to maneuver is over."
—*CHRISTOPHER NKWAYEP-CHANDO*

Acknowledgement

My deepest, warmest and everlasting thanks to Dr. Samuel F. Tchwenko and Christopher N. Chando for challenging me towards the path of humanity's enhancement.

DEDICATION

Dedicated to the loving memory of my Aunt Anna
Mapajane Chitja

The New Africa

Getting Rid of the Puppets and Dictators,
Dismantling the Anachronistic Political Systems
and Reversing the Retarding Influence of the
Mafia-style Foreign Relationships

Contents

MAPS

Africa on a map of the world

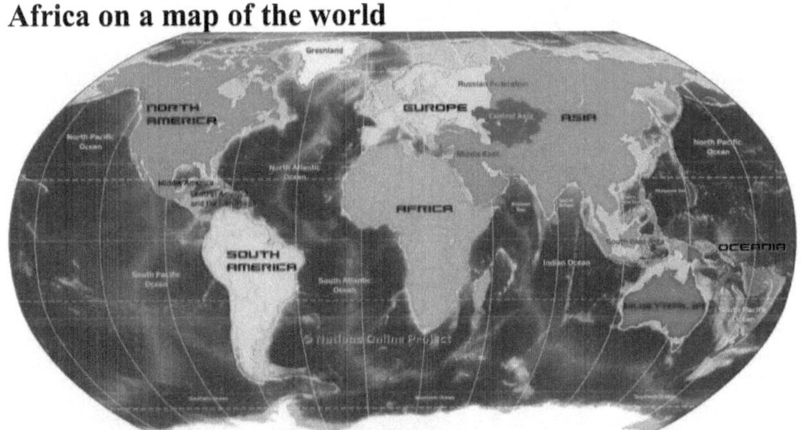

Partition map of Africa (1884-1914)

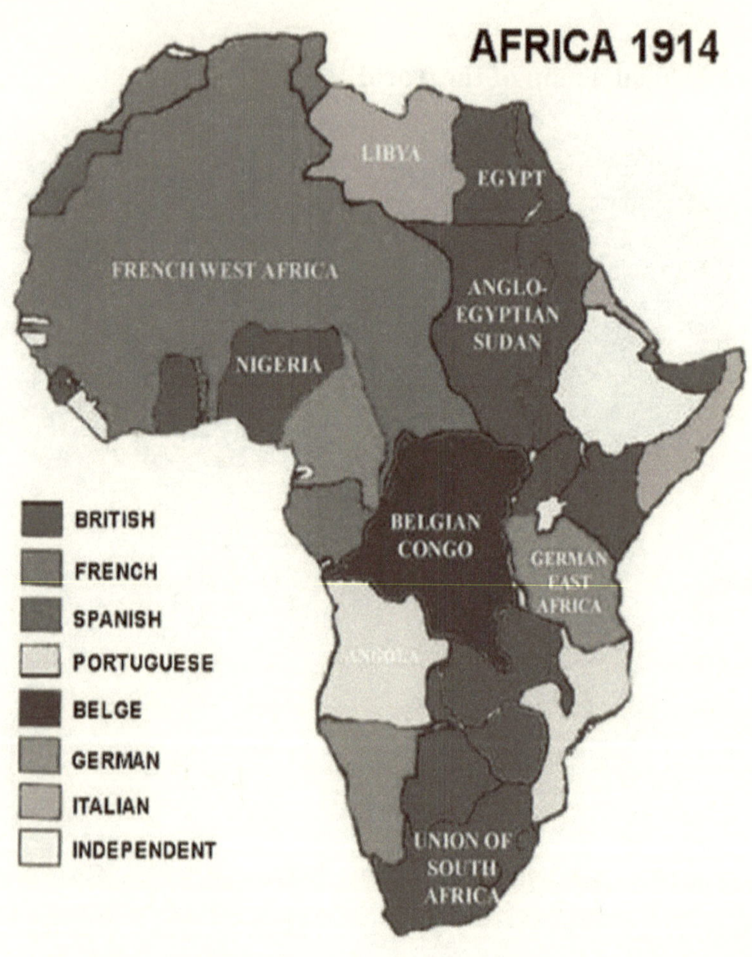

African Democracy Ratings

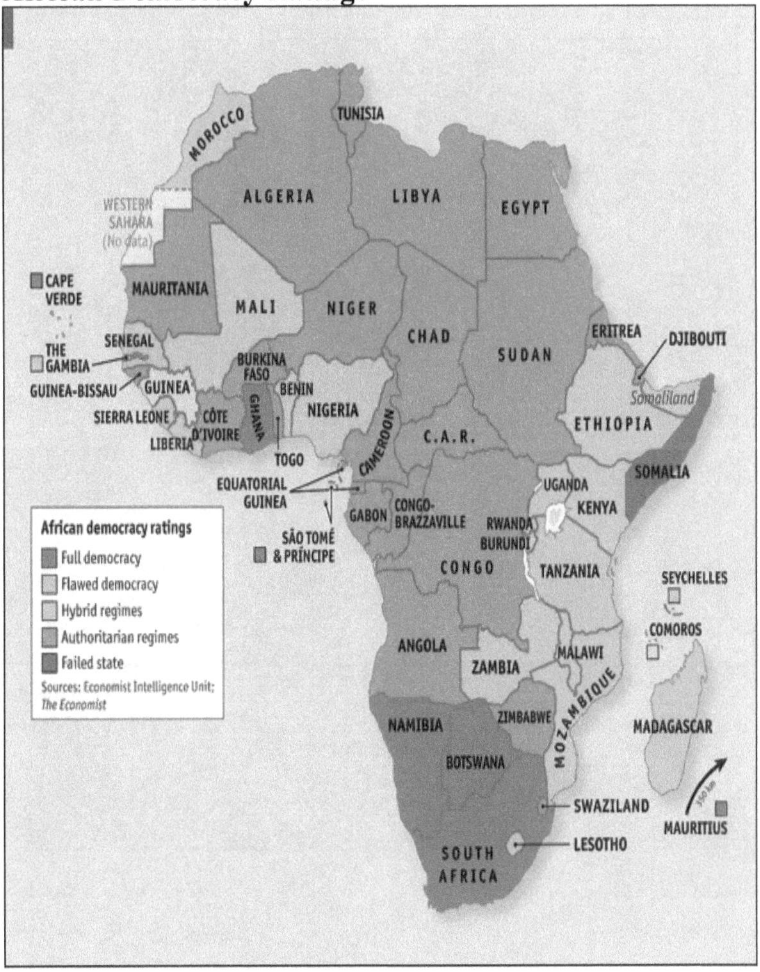

Political map of Africa

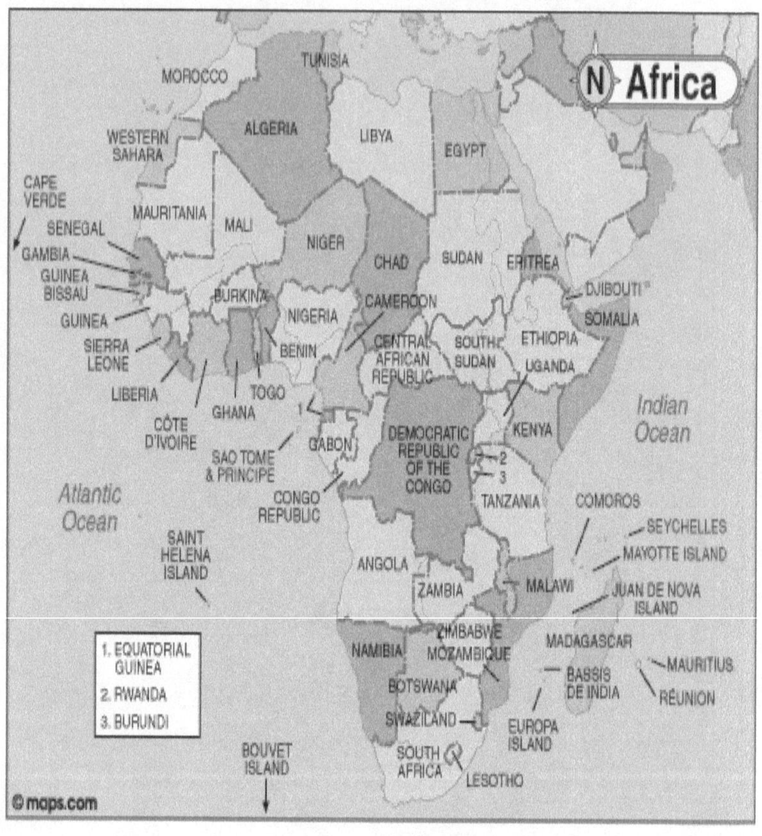

Libya on a map of Africa

Burkina Faso on a map of Africa

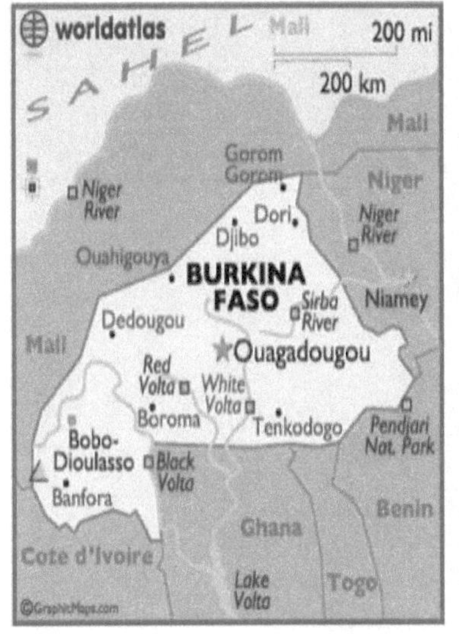

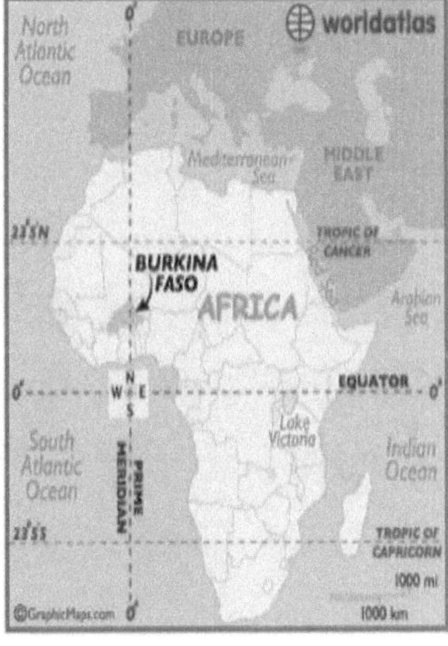

Map of Ivory Coast (Cote D'Ivoire) in Africa

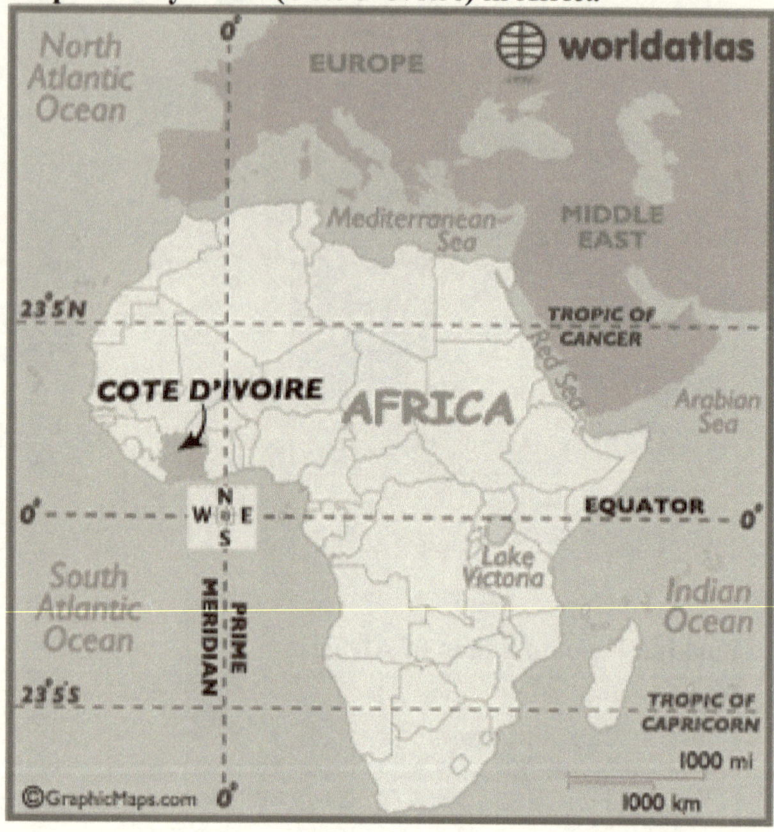

Cameroon over time

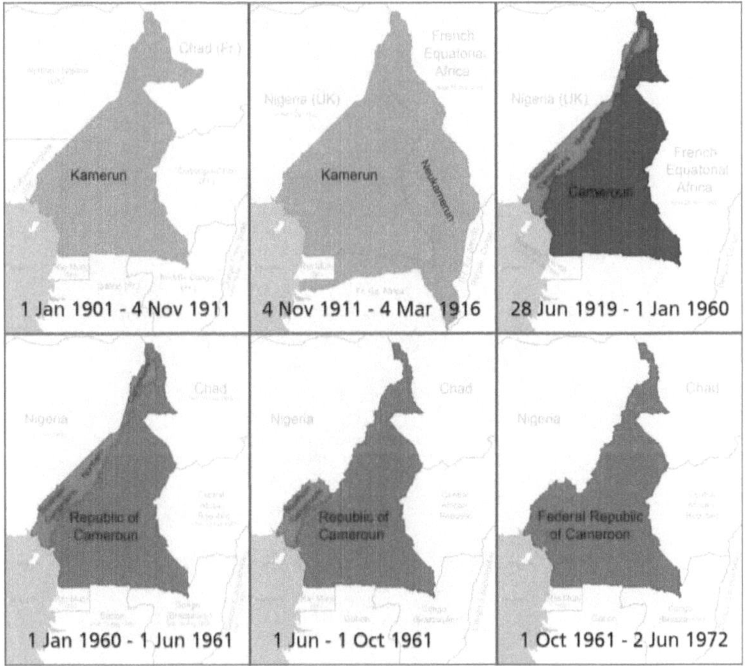

1. German Kamerun I (1884-1911)
2. German Kamerun II (1911-1916)
3. British Cameroons&French Cameroun: 1916-1960
4. British Cameroons&La Republique du Cameroun (1960-1961)
5. British Southern Cameroons&La Republique du Cameroun (1960-1961)
6. Reunited/Independent Cameroon today.

Quotes

"We find that at present the human race is divided into one wise man, nine knaves, and ninety fools out of every hundred. That is, by an optimistic observer. The nine knaves assemble themselves under the banner of the most knavish among them, and become 'politicians'; the wise man stands out, because he knows himself to be hopelessly outnumbered, and devotes himself to poetry, mathematics, or philosophy; while the ninety fools plod off under the banners of the nine villains, according to fancy, into the labyrinths of chicanery, malice and warfare. It is pleasant to have command, observes Sancho Panza, even over a flock of sheep, and that is why the politicians raise their banners. It is, moreover, the same thing for the sheep whatever the banner. If it is democracy, then the nine knaves will become members of parliament; if fascism, they will become party leaders; if communism, commissars. Nothing will be different, except the name. The fools will be still fools, the knaves still leaders, the results still exploitation. As for the wise man, his lot will be much the same under any ideology. Under democracy he will be encouraged to starve to death in a garret, under fascism he will be put in a concentration camp, under communism he will be liquidated."

T.H. White

"Cameroon is not a country of slaves that no man can free."
Janvier Chouteu-Chando

"The use of political assassination against liberation movements has changed the course of history in a number of countries in Africa and continues to devastate the Middle East. The current power relations between the Third World and the dominant Western and imperialist powers, are a product of the war of attrition which the West has waged, particularly by political assassinations, which have robbed Africa and the Middle East of some of their great leaders, and weakened their important political organizations."
Victoria Brittain

"If you are not for us, then you are against us! One day we will be living alongside you in those mansions. Your choice. Share or lose it all. We're going to take Africa away from its colonial masters. Step aside gracefully, we'll let you stay. Fight us and we'll drive you out."
Richard H. Mcbee Jr.

"You see these dictators on their pedestals, surrounded by the bayonets of their soldiers and the truncheons of their police ... yet in their hearts there is unspoken fear. They are afraid of words and thoughts: words spoken abroad, thoughts stirring at home -- all the more powerful because forbidden -- terrify them. A little mouse of thought appears in the room, and even the mightiest potentates are thrown into panic."
Winston S. Churchill

Chapter One

Blaise Compaore

Sankara and Compaoré sitting side by side in the middle

At long last, Blaise Compaore, the cold-blooded dictator of Burkina Faso, is gone, even though he has been replaced by someone of the system that France put in place. Even so, the ultimate objective of Burkinabes should be to dismantle the system and replace it with something progressive that nullifies the enslaving Colonial Pact that the Fifth Republic France led by the legendary French general and statesman Charles De Gaulle forced France's former colonies and territories in Africa to sign before allowing them to become members of the United Nations Organization through the sham process of granting them independence. These Francophone countries of Africa still find themselves trapped in a neocolonialist setup that guarantees France's interest above the interests of others, even above the interest of the home country that is the subject matter.

It is close to seven decades that most of the territories in Africa colonized by France and Britain were granted their so-called independence. But what do we discover about the former French colonies in Africa fettered by the French-imposed agreements with social, economic and political components that virtually limit the independence of these countries? Everywhere in Francophone Africa are varying combinations of instability, autocracy, semi-democracies, liberal autocracy, democracy deficits, underdevelopment, poverty, illiteracy, crime, corruption, disease and despondence.

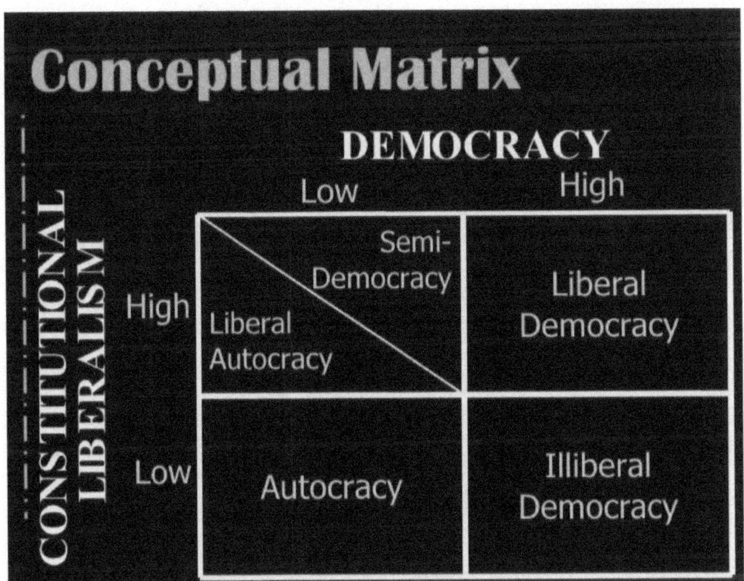

While bearing in mind the fact that the overriding objective in Burkina Faso at the moment is to create stability and dismantle the autocratic system France reimposed on this West African country after engineering the assassination of the incorruptible Thomas Sankara and his loyal associates by using the hand of Sankara's second in command, his close friend and confidante Blaise Compaore; the new political force in Burkina Faso should make as its primary and overriding long-term objective the establishment of structures that would ensure democracy, freedom, liberty, the rule of law, education, poverty reduction, transparency, economic progress, technological openness and fiscal responsibility for the country.

Most of the citizens of Burkina Faso agree that the biggest political crime committed in the history of the country was the assassination of Thomas Sankara by his successor Blaise Compaore. Yes, Blaise Compaore made it to power almost three decades ago by killing the popular former president Sankara (he was very close to him) in a French-sponsored coup over claims that Sankara was a Marxist. It was treachery at its worst, an act that not only hurt Burkina Faso's self-reliant path pursued during the four years of the Sankara presidency, but that retarded the wind of change, which Sankara's uprightness, patriotism, pan-Africanism and openness was encouraging in Africa, a wind of change apparently made unstoppable by Mikhail Gorbachev's Glasnost and Perestroika that was making dictatorships, authoritarianism and totalitarianism redundant in the world.

Furthermore, not only did Sankara's death on October 15, 1987, aged thirty seven (37), result in the extirpation of youthful steam in African politics, it also emboldened the former colonial masters and their puppets to reverse the push for democracy in Africa and drove home the message to African leaders like Jerry Rawlings of Ghana who shared similar views to Sankara that they could be next in line for elimination if they stuck with their ideas of a future Africa unshackled by foreign interests.

Almost three decades of Compaore rule has revealed that he reversed the political and social gains of Sankara's rule in favor of France, a turnaround that saw Burkina Faso going against its interest by honoring, once again, the lopsided agreement it signed with France in 1960 that completely made the West African nation a vassal of its former colonial master. In fact, it rejoined the club of Francophone African countries that were neocolonial appendages of France.

Burkina Faso's so-called benefits from this realignment during the twenty-seven (27) years that Compaore was in power are economic handouts that are making the country more reliant on France in the long run.

For Africa, Sankara's death not only traumatized the few African leaders that believed in genuine African unity, democracy, genuine African independence, an end to neocolonialism in the continent, the establishment of the rule of law in the different African countries, and in encouraging new commitments to safeguard and defend the interests of the continent and its constituent states; it discourage the young and enlightened Africans who had come to believe that the era of armed struggle to realize political change was over; and above all, it encouraged the neo-colonialists and their African puppets, most of whom have the evil disposition, to flagrantly pursue actions and policies that disregard human rights of Africans and that are devoid of planning, a sense of direction and benefits that would improve the welfare of the people.

In most countries in Francophone Africa, France and some Western governments have installed their puppets who have been in power for decades, and who during their rules, have been impoverishing their people, selling off their country's resources, saving the wealth they loot from their home countries in foreign banks (Europe and the Americas in particular). They also use some of the stolen wealth in buying properties and businesses abroad (Paul Biya of Cameroon — 36 years, the Eyademas of Togo — 5 decades, the Bongos of Gabon — 5 decades, Denis Sassou Nguesso of Congo Brazzaville — three decades etc.).

It does not come as a surprise that the people are fed up with the paralysis in their home countries, which hardly anyone disagrees, is caused by political leaderships that don't have a clue of what good governance is all about and that have no idea of what it takes to move their countries forward into the 21st century by using the human and material resources of the countries they are misruling, as well as the levers of power they usurped, power that is actually supposed to be used to make it possible for hard-working citizens to live a decent life. These puppets are in power to safeguard the benefits France gets from its former colonies as spelled out in the "Colonial Pact", which France imposed on its colonies before granting them independence in the 1960s. Books like "Triple Agent Double Cross", "Disciples of Fortune" provide a better insight.

While Burkina Faso would be remembered in African history, and more especially in Francophone African history as the first country where a Francophone African dictator was forced to step down due to a popular revolt by the masses he had been oppressing and suppressing with the help of foreign interest groups, especially the former colonial master, the events should be looked upon today as the precedence in the struggle to free Africa from tyranny, as a liberating fervor that would see the "Power of the People" confining other dictatorships like those of Paul Biya of Cameroon, the Eyademas of Togo, the Bongos of Gabon, the Kabilas of Congo-Kinshasa, Sasse Nguesso of Congo-Brazzaville, Obiang Nguema of Equatorial Guinea, Robert Mugabe of Zimbabwe, Isaias Afwerki of Eritrea, Omar Al-Bashir of Sudan, Idris Derby of Chad, Yahya Jammeh of Gambia, Yoweri Museveni of Uganda and other less vile figures in the African political scene to the dirt heaps of history.

Let us hope that African leaders who are not so vile will not turn into leeches like the aforementioned heads of state have become, while enjoying the tacit and open blessings of foreign entities, foreign powers who, in addition to safeguarding their selfish interests in their relations with these handicapped and evil dictators, could even be jubilant in thinking that these monsters calling themselves presidents or heads of state embody Africa and Africans.

The day that Paul Biya's 35-year reign, which France imposed on the Cameroonian people, will end and the anachronistic system of six decades that France imposed on Cameroon and the rest of French-speaking Africa will be dismantled, will be the beginning of true freedom, prosperity, and democracy in Francophone Africa.

Blaise Compaore was trying to emulate Paul Biya from Cameroon in his attempt to get around the two-term limit for the presidency of Burkina Faso, as set out in the constitution he approved a decade ago. He failed, but not Paul Biya from Cameroon did not. The Cameroonian president again changed his constitution in 2008, allowing him to get two more seven-year terms by holding elections that are nothing but masquerades and sacrilege for democracy, a farce he has always managed to accomplish with the open or tacit support of France, the Western Allies of France and other foreign interest groups who have always legitimized its usurpation with messages of congratulations for his victory, despite the fact that the elections were masquerades or mind-boggling farces. Even though the Cameroonian people protested and 150 were killed in February 2008, Paul Biya continued his plan and changed the constitution, then again falsified the elections in October 2011, after which he promised the Cameroonian people another victory in 2018, when he would be 85 years old. He has continued to impose himself on the people, with the support of France, the business world, and other Western governments. And today, Cameroon, one of Africa's richest countries resources-wise (human and material), is almost a bankrupt state with the highest brain drain rate in Africa and without a sense of direction.

In a world devoid of hypocrisy, human leeches like these psychopaths posing as African heads of state would not be tolerated by powers who brandish human values as the cornerstone of their advanced cultures or civilization. The time has come for the leaders of the civilized or cultured world to understand that their interests are best safeguarded in a world and more particularly in an Africa where the vast majority of the people have an interest in the progress of their countries.

Janvier Tchouteu is an Author, a political writer, and a pro-Democracy advocate. Some of his other works include "THE CANARY IN A COAL MINE EFFECT: Recent Political Assassinations That Transformed Countries, Regions and the World", "The Usurper: and Other Stories".

October 31, 2014

Chapter Two

Thomas Sankara Quotes

"While revolutionaries as individuals can be murdered, you cannot kill ideas."

"The enemy is not the one who is facing you with a sword in hand, that's the opponent. The enemy is the one behind you with a knife at your back."

"Without patriotic political education, a soldier is only a potential criminal."

I do not think that Blaise (Blaise Compaore, his deputy and best friend) wants to make an attempt on my life. The only danger is that if he refuses to act, the imperialist powers will offer him power on a silver platter by organizing my assassination. Even if they succeed in assassinating me, it does not matter! The bottom line is that they want to eat, and I am stopping them. But I shall die peacefully, for never, after what we have succeeded in instilling in the consciences of our countrymen, they cannot control our people as formerly.

"The greatest difficulty we have faced is the neocolonial way of thinking that exists in this country. We were colonized by a country, France, that left us with certain habits. For us, being successful in life, being happy, meant trying to live as they do in France, like the richest of the French."

"You cannot carry out fundamental change without a certain amount of madness. In this case, it comes from nonconformity, the courage to turn your back on the old formulas, the courage to invent the future."

"Debt is a cleverly managed reconquest of Africa. It is a reconquest that turns each one of us into a financial slave."

"Let there be an end to the arrogance of the big powers who miss no opportunity to put the rights of the people in question. Africa's absence from the club of those who have the right to veto is unjust and should be ended."

We are not against progress, but we do not want progress that is anarchic and criminally neglects the rights of others."

"Inequality can be done away with only by establishing a new society, where men and women will enjoy equal rights…Thus, the status of women will improve only with the elimination of the system that exploits them."

"The spirit is smothered, as it were, by ignorance, but as soon as ignorance is destroyed, the spirit shines forth like the sun when it breaks through clouds."

"The patriarchal family made its appearance, founded on the sole and personal property of the father, who had become head of the family. Within this family, the woman was oppressed."

"I want people to remember me as someone whose life has been helpful to humanity."

"Our country produces enough to feed us all. Alas, for lack of organization, we are forced to beg for food aid. It's this aid that instills in our spirits the attitude of beggars."

"Everything that man can imagine, he is capable of creating."

"It took the madmen of yesterday for us to be able to act with extreme clarity today. I want to be one of those madmen. We must dare to invent the future."

Thomas Sankara

When Africa woke up that morning of October 16, 1987, and learned of the death of Thomas Sankara, the charismatic head of state of Burkina Faso, shock, grief and melancholy settled over the continent. When more news sipped in reporting that he was killed along with twelve others in a coup led by the then Vice President Blaise Compaoré, (who after the coup became the president and ruled until his ouster in a popular uprising in October 31, 2014), the Burkina Faso masses were outraged. Thomas Sankara had made known to the world that Blaise Compaoré was his chum and closest confidant.

Sankara and Compaoré sitting side by side in the middle

So, who was this young man who took a landlocked country in Africa out of an impasse, a territory that was the heartland of the Songhai Empire, and then showed the people there and their brethren in the rest of Africa the path to a future devoid of the retarding influence of neocolonialism?

The story begins in 1949, with the birth of Thomas Sankara on December 21 of that year in Yako, Upper Volta, and became legendary with his death on Oct 15, 1987 in Ouagadougou, Burkina Faso from the bullets of his assassins. However, we shall deal with the chapters that constitute his life on earth as we delve deeper into how he became the leader of the Burkinabe Revolution before his untimely death.

Sankara's rise to the highest office of the land began following his training as a pilot and after he became a captain in the Upper Volta Air Force. But it wasn't only his skills as a pilot that made him a popular figure in the country's capital city called Ouagadougou, especially after fighting in the 1974 border war against Mali. The fact that he was a decent guitarist and the fact that he liked motorbikes may also have contributed to his charisma. So, his appointment as Secretary of State for Information in 1981 by Colonel Saye Zerbo, who became the president of the country after ending the 14-year rule of Sangoulé Lamizana with a coup d'état on 25 November 1980, was welcomed by the country folks. However, when he resigned from the government on 21 April 1982, citing the regime's anti-labor drift, the population saw another laudable side of his character that was uncommon around. He was incorruptible.

The November 07, 1982 coup d'état led by Maj. Dr. Jean-Baptiste Ouédraogo and the Council of Popular Salvation (CSP) that overthrew Colonel Saye Zerbo brought about a resuscitation of Sankara's fortunes when the new president made him Prime minister in 1983. But then, Jean-Christophe Mitterrand, the son of French president Francois Mitterrand who happened to be his father's African Affairs adviser, visited Upper Volta that year, did not like the young Sankara's political ideas, bluntness and incorruptible nature, and so made the Upper Voltan president place Sankara and some of his close associates under house arrest. His confinement by the authorities triggered a popular uprising that could not be contained.

The Sankara saga would not have taken new dimensions had a group of men in Upper Volta, known today as Burkina Faso, not decided to launch a revolution that would enable the country "to accept the responsibility of its reality and its destiny with human dignity". A Coup d'état organized by Blaise Compaoré organized with the help of Captain Henri Bongo, Major Jean-Baptiste Booker Lingam and the charismatic Captain Thomas Sankara deposed Jean-Baptiste Ouedraogo on 4 August 1983, after which they pronounced Thomas Sankara the leader. The 33-year old Sankara went on to become a prominent figure in the group of African leaders who wanted to give the continent in general, and their countries in particular, a new socio-political dimension devoid of the shackles of neocolonialism, especially the overbearing French control of its former African colonies and territories.

Thomas Sankara, the charismatic left-leaning leader of a country in the heart of West Africa was sometimes nicknamed "Tom Sank" and was considered by some of his admirers as an "African Che Guevara" even before he became the head of state of the country following the coup masterminded by his friend Blaise Compaoré.

A year after assuming the highest office in the land,

Sankara began the most ambitious programs for social and economic change ever attempted in any of the countries on the African continent. He changed the name of the country from Upper Volta to Burkina Faso, meaning "the land of upright people" in Mossi and Dyula, which are the country's two major languages. He also came up with a new flag and a new anthem for the enthusiastic country.

The young president would orient the country's policy towards fighting corruption, reforestation, averting famine, and towards the making of education and healthcare real priorities for the nation.

His domestic policies focused on:

- preventing famine with agrarian self-sufficiency and land reform that resulted in food self-sufficiency three years into his presidency
- making education a priority, which the government was relentless in pursuing through a nationwide literacy campaign
- and promoting public health by vaccinating 2, 500, 000 (2.5 million) children against meningitis, yellow fever and measles.

Other laudable aspects of his national agenda included:
- the planting of over 10, 000, 000 (ten million) trees, which went a long way in halting the growing desertification of the Sahel
- the doubling of wheat production by redistributing land from feudal landlords to peasants

- the suspension of rural poll taxes and domestic rents
- and the launch of an ambitious road and railway construction program to "tie the nation together".

At the local level, Sankara also led the drive for every village to build a medical dispensary, and for over 350 communities to build schools using their own labor.

Right after he came to power, he became the champion of women's emancipation and rights in Africa. In fact, this was confirmed by his ban on female genital mutilation; his abolition of forced marriages, child marriages and polygamy; as well as by his policies and efforts encouraging women to take up leadership positions in the government and society, especially by appointing women to high governmental positions, and encouraging them to work outside the home and to stay in school, even if they became pregnant. When he wrote that:

"The revolution and women's liberation go together.
We do not talk of women's emancipation as an act of charity or because of a surge of human compassion.
It is a basic necessity for the triumph of the revolution. Women hold up the other half of the sky."

It was a reflection of his determination to increase the lot of women in his country and Africa.

Sankara pursued a foreign policy that did not condone imperialism and encouraged cooperation based on respect and the recognition of Burkina Faso's interests as well as the interest of the other parties dealing with Burkina Faso.

This saw his government eschewing all foreign aid, pushing for debt reduction in an audacious manner, nationalizing all land and mineral wealth, thereby averting the power and influence of the International Monetary Fund (IMF) and its sister financial institution the World Bank.

Even though Sankara's revolutionary programs for self-reliance transformed him into an icon in the eyes of many of Africa's poor and increased his popularity with most of the impoverished citizens of Burkina Faso, his policies undermined the vested interests of a wide range of groups (the Francophile Burkinabe middle-class, the tribal leaders who resented the fact that he stripped them of their long-held traditional privileges to forced labor and payment of tributes, and France and its ally the Ivory Coast under Félix Houphouet-Boigny, whom he considered a puppet of France). So, when Blaise Compaoré orchestrated his overthrow and assassination on 15 October 1987, many people (Burkinabes and non-Burkinabes) were left wondering whether he did not see it coming. After all, a week before his assassination, he declared that:

"While revolutionaries as individuals can be murdered, you cannot kill ideas."

His intuition was at play all right, but he did not seem to be the type that was prepared to go through the horrors of investigating and eliminating those he had been working closely with. He, like many great figures in history, understood that betrayal from those close to you is not the fault of the betrayed, especially if the leader never harbored evil intentions against his associates or comrades.

When the news of Thomas Sankara's assassination on October 15, 1987 went out shortly after he and twelve other officials were killed in a coup d'état organized by his former colleague Blaise Compaoré, it was received with outrage, sadness, apprehension and disbelief in all of the countries of the world. But nowhere was the grief as great as in Burkina Faso and the rest of Africa where he was regarded by the masses as the beacon of hope in a continent dominated by leaders with the evil disposition, most of whom were puppets of foreign powers. Blaise Compaoré not only made sure Sankara got buried in an unmarked grave, he desecrated Sankara's legacy even further by reversing most of his policies and by realigning Burkina Faso with those foreign leaders and countries that were hostile to Sankara, especially the former colonial master France. Many people versed with history wasted no time in comparing Blaise Compaoré to the Brutus (Marcus Julius Brutus), a politician of the Roman Republic who participated in the assassination of his close friend the Roman Emperor Julius Caesar.

The fact that Blaise Compare would have Henri Zongo and Jean-Baptiste Boukary Lingani, whom he had initially been ruling with in a triumvirate, arrested, charged with plotting to overthrow the government, summarily tried, and then executed in September 1989, proved that Sankara was a trusting and trusted member in that group that seized power in 1983 and began the Burkinabe Revolution.

Sankara's quest to realize the most ambitious programs for social and economic change ever attempted on the

African continent ended up as a partially realized dream, but one that is appreciated for stirring the hopes of the African youth. Today, he is a legend in his country and Africa thirty years after his death.

Antonio de Figueiredo, a journalist, activist and broadcaster who campaigned for the liberation of Portugal's African colonies, and who did more than anyone to bring the issue of colonial oppression in Angola, Mozambique, Guinea and Cape Verde to the attention of the English-speaking world, understood the magnitude of Thomas Sankara's influence when he wrote in February 2008 that:

"Africa and the world are yet to recover from Sankara's assassination. Just as we have yet to recover from the loss of Patrice Lumumba, Kwame Nkrumah, Eduardo Mondlane, Amílcar Cabral, Steve Biko, Samora Machel, and most recently John Garang, to name only a few. While malevolent forces have not used the same methods to eliminate each of these great pan-Africanists, they have been guided by the same motive: to keep Africa in chains."

Thomas Sankara, the revolutionary and short-lived head of state of Burkina Faso who reduced his salary to $450 dollars, sold the government's Mercedes Benz fleet, banned the allocation of chauffeurs for government officials and made the Renault 5 the official car, was commemorated in ceremonies that took place in Burkina Faso, Mali, Senegal, Niger, Tanzania, Burundi, France, Canada and the United States on 15 October

2007, twenty years after his assassination. He was exhumed in 2015, one year after the popular uprising that chased Blaise Compare out of power.

Today, numerous books, articles and other works of arts glorify the selfless African legend who took upon himself the colossal task of putting the people on their feet and showing them the path to a future devoid of neocolonialist influence that is wrapped up in trade, finance and imported cultures that undermine the strength of African communalist values and the sacredness of the family.

Chapter Three

"If we fight to the death against an arbitrary integration of our country into the French colonial empire, it is because we want to remain the conquering defenders of the right of peoples to self-determination. We are thus, in the service of Kamerun and Africa ... we are the true craftsmen of international detente. As revolutionary nationalists, we are fighing to realize for the Kamerun and for it alone, a true national "Independence" with "Unification" as a precondition, simultaneous or consecutive, but never excluded.

Ruben Um Nyobè

"We are not involved in this struggle only because we think that we will dismantle this system in the course of our life. We hope Cameroon changes tomorrow. But if it doesn't, we will be happy to know that we made the ground fertile for the next generation that will end the rot in this country, and then establish the "NEW CAMEROON"."

Dr. Samuel F. Tchwenko, former UPCist and chief ideologue of the historic SDF of 1990-2002

Paul Biya

Pose this question to any Cameroonian with a deep perception of the world: Who is Africa's most dishonest and illusionary head of state? The answer from the absolute majority would be obvious. Our tenant in the unity palace is that head of state.

Cameroon's second president is a bad leader in the furthest sense of the word. His governance has destroyed most of the foundations of our people's way of life and progressive values. Unprincipled, unscrupulous and visionless, he was elusive enough during his early years of leadership by convincing many to regard him as a brilliant leader. Yes, he made himself brilliant and appealing to the people even despite his true convictions.

The second Cameroonian president as the demagogue he is, harangued about his NEW DEAL of Rigor and Moralization, when he never intended to work for the interest of all Cameroonians. He came to power for the sole purpose of defending the interest of his patron(The mafia in the French establishment over its African policy), to enhance the material well-being and social position of his clique of unscrupulous businessmen, politicians, functionaries and above all the ethnic group of his birth.

A second Cameroonian president is a dishonorable man without convictions. He began his political manifestations as a Cameroonian nationalist of socialist orientation under the banner of the Union of the Populations of Cameroon (UPC), but soon unhesitatingly discarded his nationalist garment for the high positions offered to renegades of the Cameroonian struggle by the Anglophobic Ahidjo regime and its French masters. Having switched his loyalty to the glory of naked power in the French-backed regime overseeing the genocide of the union-nationalist forces in Cameroon, Paul Biya quickly won the hearts of his patron to become prime minister in 1972 and later president in 1982. After that, he shed all aspects of his ties to Cameroonian nationalism and became a fervent Francophile and Anglophone manipulator. Today, it is clear for all to see that Paul Biya stands as the leader of the renegade forces that may eventually kill Cameroonian nationalism and lead the nation into the abyss, denying it the realization of its century-old Cameroonian dream of unity, independence, prosperity and open opportunities. He is a purposeless, faceless and paranoiac leader whose long years of power and the emptiness of his rule have been masked by France and his Cameroonian collaborators.

During his early years as head of state, Paul Biya talked of rigor in the implementation of progressive work ethics, rules, laws, freedom, Human rights and economic reforms, when he never intended to see the slightest change in the French imposed system he inherited from his predecessor. Biya never had any intention to change the course of dictatorship, corruption, kleptomania, and division that was the rule of the system and the trappings of power and wealth it offered. A decade after his pronouncement of rigor, Cameroon which had the second fastest economic growth rate in the world after South Korea in 1986(though it lagged behind its true potentials even then), is today with the least promising economy in Africa.

Biya's moralization rhetoric is an unacceptable abuse to humanity. Promising to make his rule a moral one where governance would be based on a program to enhance the right conducts in public, social, economic and political affairs, he reneged by presiding over the worst degeneration of a non-war ravaged nation in Africa.

Unfortunately, for Cameroonians, Biya is one of those regrettable products of nature with quite an exceptional strength of character that is a negation of a good leadership. It does not bother him in the least that his practically wrong actions and leadership have reduced Cameroonians into a poverty-stricken people, eroded their sense of purpose, divided their ranks, rendered them into the grips of despondence, denigrated their influence in national and international politics, and encouraged corruption to the form of an art; and above all, it suits his propose that he has wrapped Cameroon into the clutch and whims of France.

After becoming the president in 1982, Biya has ruled Cameroon more like an absentee caretaker than even an absentee landlord. A two-month trip abroad for amusement using the taxpayer's money is unprecedented from any head of state. Nevertheless, it surprises only those who have no insight into his personality. Biya committed moral suicide years ago and now lacks the morality that is expected from a head of state. His rule has shattered the bilateral respect that prevailed between the different generations.

From peasant origins, Biya has learned, but wrongly assimilated aristocratic values. The sad result of this is his blatant and unjustifiable contempt of the masses from where he had his origins. As a man of high learning, it is unfortunate that despite his long years of service in the system, he still possesses all the traits of a pseudo-intellectual and a pedant. And it is due to his awareness of his intellectual feebleness that he has developed a masked inferiority complex. That is why he rejects, snubs and shies away from the good ideas of his intellectual superiors.

Cameroon is the only nation in Africa where its true liberation fighters and nationalists were never permitted to the helm of power. It is the first nation in Africa where France became deeply involved in collaboration with Ahidjo, in the genocide of those who resisted its deception (close to a million deaths in the 1956-1970 war against the UPC). Cameroon is the only country in Africa, which has been the most cruelly raped in our modern times by France. Even though Cameroonians are one of the most dynamic people in the continent, they have never been left to their devices to harness their potentials and build their country into the great nation that it truly deserves. Instead, Cameroonians have been brought low by a conspiracy hatched during the years of Jacques Foccart's control of French policy on Africa, a conspiracy that has effectively used Cameroonian collaborators, especially Paul Biya.

It does not bother the second Cameroonian president in the least that the Cameroonian people are suffocating in his bondage. He has lost touch with the Cameroonian masses, the Cameroonian reality, and life in its different forms. However, unlike his psychopathic counterpart, the Roman emperor Nero, he has mastered one art—the art of retaining power despite the opposition from the masses. And as most megalomaniacs and experimentalists, he would continue to experiment with his theory of power retention, despite his unpopularity, not worried that the Cameroonian people are being dragged into the abyss in the process.

Biya is performing his theory of power retention on us, an experiment that will go a long way to destroy the best of our creative forces if left to persist. Moreover, with that will be the destruction of the faith we have in our dream and worst still the mother of progress, which is hope. The sad result of the disaster of Biya's rule would be the death of Cameroon. To the rational mind, that is unacceptable.

Perhaps for a little while longer, the living specter of the second Cameroonian president will continue to haunt the people—treacherous in his ways, ruthless in his methods and nonchalant in his views. It is our unavoidable task, if only for the sake of our children, that we rise up— take back our dignity, hope and future from him and his patrons. Then following the natural course of history, we shall confine him and his legacy to the dustbin of history.

February 28, 1995   *Janvier Tchouteu*

Chapter Four

"A people determined to fight for freedom and independence is invincible."
Ruben Um Nyobè

"Cameroon is not a country of slaves that no man can free."
Janvier Chouteu-Chando

"Until the lions have their own historians, the history of the hunt will always glorify the hunter."
Chinua Achebe

"The characters in our other lives are ghosts that literature is reviving."
Olivier Weber

Félix-Roland Moumié

UPC Leaders (L. to R.) front row: Castor Osendé Afana, Abel Kingué, Ruben Um Nyobé, Félix Moumié, and Ernest Ouandié

Born in 1926, Félix-Roland Moumié was an anti-colonialist Cameroonian leader and Pan-Africanist. His assassination in Geneva on November 03, 1960 by William Bechtel of the SDECE (the French Secret Service) with thallium is regarded as the most brazen crime committed by the French secret service abroad, and perhaps the biggest single blow suffered by Cameroonian civic-nationalists fighting for the liberation of the land from French neocolonial control.

Dr. Felix-Roland Moumié was the head of the UPC (*Union des Populations du Cameroun,* also called *Union du Peuple Camerounais*—"Union of the Populations of Cameroon") from 1958-1960. The UPC was the first historic political party to emerge from the territories of the former German colony of Kamerun. Founded in 1948, the UPC operated in both French Cameroun and British Cameroons—Trust Territories that emerged from the 1884-1916 former German Kamerun following its partition between Britain and France as agreed in the June 28, 1919 Treaty of Versailles, the most important of the peace treaties that brought World War I to a close by formalizing the end of the state of war between Germany and the Allied Powers. The party's primary objective was the reunification and independence of British Cameroons and French Cameroun, Trust Territories that were the successors of the League of Nations mandates, and that came into being when the League of Nations ceased to exist in 1946.

The French Trusteeship administration banned the UPC in 1955, accusing it of fomenting civil unrest, thereby forcing the party into exile in the summer of 1955.

However, The UPC resurfaced in 1956 and challenged France via the international media. The British colonial authorities also banned the UPC in British Cameroons in 1958, thereby forcing most of its leadership that escaped French Cameroun and sought sanctuary in British Cameroons, to flee to Egypt, Ghana, China, and other countries that were supportive of the Cameroonian cause for its reunification and independence.

Ruben Um Nyobé, the party's leader and Secretary General; Ernest Ouandié and Abel Kingué, the party's two vice presidents; and Felix Moumié pledged to carry on with the struggle for the reunification and independence of French Cameroun and British Cameroons, despite France's resolve to divide and rule the peoples of the former German Kamerun. After all, the UPC commanded the support of most the people of French Cameroun, and its offshoots and sister parties in British Cameroons commanded the support of the electorate there. In fact, more than 80% of educated Cameroonians supported the party and its cause for the reunification and independence of the lands of the former German Kamerun.

However, the party received its first major trauma when three years after the ban, at a time that some pundits were beginning to think that France would allow the party to start operating again as a legal political entity, the security forces of the French Trusteeship administration assassinated the UPC's first historic leader Ruben Um Nyobé on September 13, 1958, near his home village of Boumnyebel in the Bassaland.

So, when Dr. Felix-Roland Moumié succeeded Ruben

Um Nyobé, he was forced to operate from exile, even though the UPC was the only party in French Cameroun that enjoyed the overwhelming support of French Camerounians, and even though it was also the only political party in that part of the former German Kamerun that shared a similar program with sister parties or offshoots in British Cameroons. Undeterred, he challenged France's crackdown on the UPC in a more determined manner, so that UPC partisans were in control of much the countryside of the southern half of French Cameroun before France handed French Cameroun's political control or sovereignty to its puppet Ahmadou Ahidjo, declared the land independent on January 01, 1960, and at the same time concluded a series of socio-economic and political agreements with the infant state that virtually made it a backyard of France.

Considered by some as the "African Che Guevara in the making", Félix Moumié was an astute leader as well as a great organizer who before his death, had met that summer of 1960 with Ernesto Che Guevara, the Argentine international revolutionary and second-in-command in the new anti-American and anti-Western government of Fidel Castro's Cuba. In addition to that development, the Cameroonian partisan leader had successfully developed a special rapport with the bellicose Egyptian president Gamal Abdel Nasser, the Pan-Africanist president of Ghana Kwame Nkrumah, the unwavering Patrice Lumumba of Congo-Kinshasa (the former Belgian Congo), and the stubborn nationalist Guinean head of state Sékou Touré who defied France and whisked Guinea out of the neocolonial clutches of its former colonial master.

Many pundits think France and its Cold-War allies feared the new UPC leader's drive in forging strong relationships with some of the other leaders in the communist bloc who hoped to see Africa emerge one day as an economically united and politically integrated continent. The fact that those leaders promised to increase their support to Moumié's partisan group made France and Ahmadou Ahidjo extremely nervous.

The exiled second leader of the Cameroonian civic-nationalist movement was on a mission to Europe in October 1960, when William Bechtel invited him to dinner in a hotel in Geneva, Switzerland, posing as a journalist. In fact, he was a member of the "Main Rouge," an offshoot of a special unit in the French secret service charged with eliminating anti-French and pro-independence African nationalists and their supporters in Europe.

Distracted by a summon to the phone by a restaurant staff, Moumié left his unfinished drink that Bechtel contaminated by pouring a lethal dose of thallium into it. But Moumié did not drink it upon his return. So, Bechtel created another distraction, during which he poured another dose of thallium into Moumié's wine. Moumié ended up gulping down both drinks and died in a Geneva hospital on November 3, 1960, days before his return to Guinea, and much earlier than his killers had planned. The fact that the Cameroonian liberation leader took an overdose of the poison thwarted the plot France had hatched to blame Felix Moumié's death on Guinean president Sekou Touré, who had been acting as the UPC leader's host during his exile in the Guinean capital of Conakry.

Félix Moumié's assassination would be followed three months later by the horrendous assassination of Patrice Lumumba of the former Belgian Congo. The deaths of these two African civic-nationalists with a Pan-Africanist vision would be followed by a bloody repression of the popular resistance to the neo-colonial regimes in their respective countries.

With the execution of Félix Moumié's successor Ernest Ouandie in January 1971, the neo-colonial counter offensive against the anti-colonialist movements in the heart of Africa would be over, spelling victory for the neo-colonial forces. This new reality would have disastrous consequences not only in the Central African region but throughout Africa. Francophone Sub-Saharan Africa has not dared to oppose French neocolonialism since the defeat of Cameroonian civic-nationalism and France's imposition of a mafia-like system of control over its former colonies that makes use of French puppets who are not accountable to their people.

The death of Félix Moumié, the retention of the French ban on the UPC, the UPC's 1958 expulsion from British Cameroons, and the return to power in France of the French legend and neocolonialist General Charles De Gaulle made the realization of the Kamerunian dream of reunification, independence and development seem impossible. However, offshoots of the UPC in British Cameroons and the Cameroonian civic-nationalists in British Southern Cameroons realized the reunification dream by championing the campaign in the United Nations sponsored plebiscite or referendum for the vote to reunite British Southern Cameroons with the one-year old Republic of Cameroun, the former French Cameroun that got its independence on January 01, 1960 under the anti-UPC government of the French puppet Ahmadou Ahidjo.

In fact, even though inferiorly armed, the UPC led an effective guerilla campaign that had at the end of 1959, confined complete French control in the south of the country only to the cities and towns, leaving the villages and countryside under the control of the UPC. And since the UN Trusteeship Agreement set a cap to the number of troops the French Army could have in the territory, France decided to precipitate the granting of independence to French Cameroon. However, it granted French Cameroun independence on January 01, 1960 under its puppet Ahmadou Ahidjo, and at the same time compelled Ahidjo to sign a secretive pact with France, an agreement with economic, political and military components that among other things, allowed France to multiply the number of French troops it had stationed in the former French Cameroun, called the Republic of Cameroon thereafter. The French army would reinforce its presence in the land by increasing the number of its soldiers and hardware there, and by speeding up the recruitment and training of a French-led local Cameroonian Army. These Franco-Cameroonian armies would defeat the insurgents in its major strongholds in the Bassaland in 1960 and in the Bamilekeland from 1962-1964, by inflicting heavy losses on the UPC and the civilian populations through their indiscriminate bombing of both the guerilla camps and the civil communities, a scorch-earth policy per se that some historians and various pundits consider a French-led genocide against certain forces and populations of areas of Cameroon that opposed France's neocolonialist plans for Cameroon.

By 1965, it was realized that the UPC could no longer win the armed conflict against the French Army and the Cameroonian Army France created for the puppet Ahmadou Ahidjo regime. Prevaricated efforts at achieving peace through peace talks would lure Felix Moumié's successor Ernest Ouandie out of the bush, leading to his surrender/capture/, and then execution in January 1971, thereby ending the UPC armed struggle against France for the reunification, independence and freedom of the territories of the former German Kamerun, a conflict that resulted in the deaths of more than half a million Cameroonian lives in what some pundits view as "Cameroon's Unfinished Liberation", since those and the heirs of those who campaigned and fought for Cameroon's reunification and independence have been prevented from power in the country ever since.

Cameroonians from the English-speaking part of the reunited Cameroon soon realized that they had been deceived and subjugated by France and her puppet, like the defeated and subdued populations of the French-speaking part of the country, and that they too were now under the suffocating yoke of a French-imposed system managed by the dictatorship of France's puppet Ahmadou Ahidjo. Paul Biya, another French marionette and Ahmadou Ahidjo's successor from the orders of France, has been in power since 1982 and has exacerbated the suffocation of Cameroon even further. Close to sixty years after, Cameroon is still under the control of the anti-UPC forces put in place by France—these are Cameroonians who played no role, whether as moderates or as radicals, in the nationalist struggle for the land's reunification and independence. In fact, France aided its puppets in establishing a police state in order to impose their rule, which explains why Cameroon has never experienced rule under a head of state that is or was the choice of the people.

The mafia continues. The country that embodies Africa's daring spirit is still in the grips of the forces that were against its quest for liberation, development and partnership with other progressive forces of the world.

The assassinations of Ruben Um Nyobé, Félix Moumié, Patrice Lumumba, Castor Osendé Afana, Ernest Ouandie and tens of thousands of Congolese and Cameroonian civic-nationalists was after all a successful campaign by neocolonial powers to destroy Africa's genuine independent development, as defeating the anti-colonial movements in these countries weakened the pan-Africanist drive to create an African economic union and to integrate the continent politically. In spite of any indications or expectations to the contrary, the Cameroon of Nyobe/Moumié/Ouandie that was never realized, and the Congo of Lumumba that failed to be, would have been at the geographic, economic and political center of the African Union that is still the vision of many progressive Africans who hope to see the continent secure a place of respect for itself in the growing multi-polar world.

Today, Félix Moumié's sarcophagus is still missing in what was his resting place in the cemetery in Conakry, Guinea.   Albert Kingue is still buried in Cairo, Egypt. Ruben Um Nyobé, Ernest Ouandie, Castor Osendé Afana, and the other leaders of the UPC killed by the Franco-Ahidjo forces are hardly acknowledged, let alone recognized in the annals of Cameroonian history, even though their names grace streets and infrastructures in other countries of Africa and the world.

Six decades after, Cameroonians rising up to challenge the mafia state still see Felix-Roland Moumié and the other historic Union-Nationalist leaders that got killed, exiled or undermined by France and the puppets it imposed on the country, as the forces to emulate in their drive to dismantle the system imposed on the people. The system and its authoritarian political establishment is today led Paul Biya, a puppet imposed by France on the people of Cameroon. The second Cameroonian president has been in power for forty-five years (thirty-five years as the president or head of state, and ten years as prime minister of the only country in Africa where its head of state has never been the choice of the people, but rather an imposition by neocolonialists).

Chapter Five

"...The world gets blessed every now and then with unique souls who though burdened by their invisible crosses, still have the extraordinary strength to forge ahead in life and give others a helping hand at the same time. Despite their tribulations, most of us think they are fine. Even when the weight of their crosses become unbearable, even when they proceed in a breathless manner, we still have a hard time understanding that they are drowning. In fact, we even condemn them for failing to sacrifice more..."

Janvier Chouteu-Chando, Disciples of Fortune

A specter looms in the lives of every Cameroonian child, man or woman. It is the living president of the land in the middle of Africa, the land that is often referred to as the microcosm of the continent. The specter is President Paul Biya of Cameroon. When rumors spread like wildfire in June 2004 that he had just died, there were widespread scenes of jubilation all across the half a million square kilometer landmass called Cameroon. Days after the circulation of the unverified account, he returned home from abroad where he had been passing his time, intermittently, about six months every year for over two decades, and then declared to the sycophants waiting to receive him at the airport that there would be a …. "Rendez-vous in 20 years' time with those who wish me dead…"

Cameroonians were not the only ones who disbelieved him when he made that pronouncement among other things. Many of those who follow political developments in the world in general, and in Africa and Cameroon in particular, marveled at his audacity. After all, more than 80% of the Cameroonian population loathed his rule; he was already in power for more than two decades as the head of state, after having been the country's prime minister (1972-1982) or the second most powerful person in the system put in place in Cameroon by the French overlords.

But Paul Biya proved everyone wrong. He pulled off another electoral charade and declared himself the winner in the October 2004 presidential election, and then changed his constitution in 2008 that would allow him to run for two more presidential 7-year terms (despite the deaths of 150 protesting Cameroonians caused by his armed forces), meaning that he could be president until the year 2025 (a record of 43 years in power) when he would be 92 years of age.

That explains why by the time Paul Biya held another masquerade called presidential elections in October 2011, he had already successfully humbled the internationally recognized opposition heads (who are all former members of the country's sole political party from 1972-1990, a party Biya has been leading since 1984), promised to give them positions in his government and made it known in plain terms that the system string-controlled by the puppeteer (France) would never allow political change in Cameroon that would curtail France's unrestricted interests in the African country.

The octogenarian Paul Biya is variously described as the Maradona (he fakes and wins elections just like Maradona faked and scored a goal in his "Hand of God" goal) of Cameroonian and African politics, the master of presidential patricide (he devoured his predecessor who passed over power to him, leading to the first Cameroonian president Ahmadou Ahidjo's exile, death and burial abroad—Senegal), the absentee president, the vindictive president, the evil president, etc. etc.

As a German colony from 1884-1916, Kamerun was often referred to by the German Colonial administration and the imperial-minded in the Kaiser's Germany as an "African Pearl", owing to the colony's robust economy, highest literacy rate in the continent in the early 1900s, magnificent physical features, rich and varied vegetation cover, and also owing to its diverse ethnic ethnicities that included all the major language groups in Africa (Afro-Asia, Niger-Congo-A, Niger-Congo-B or Bantu, and Nilo-Saharan. in fact, historians consider the German colony of Kamerun as a major part of Adolf Hitler's rue over the territories Germany lost after the First World because of the peace terms imposed on it by the victories Allied Powers during the Versailles Conference. As it happens, one of the peace terms imposed on the post-Kaiser Germany was the loss of German Kamerun to Britain and France. That was how Kamerun was partitioned into British Cameroons and French Cameroon.

As a matter of fact, the French Cameroun mandate became France's most valuable assets in Sub-Saharan Africa. Its value was validated even further when the territory became the Launchpad of French General Charles De Gaulle-led Free French Forces that wrestled French Equatorial Africa from the Nazi puppet regime of Vichy France during the Second World War. This force would gallantly fight alongside Allied Forces against Italian and German forces in Libya, Tunisia and the Middle East, before carrying on to Italy and France where their biggest achievement was the liberation of Paris. The fact that French Camerounians played an invaluable role in the war effort to liberate France from Nazi Germany makes the explanation simple as to why French Camerounian soldiers returned home and sought self-government, liberty, democracy, reunification with British Cameroons that would culminate in the independence of the two United Nations Trust Territories. They were merely seeking the rights that they had helped France to regain from Nazi Germany, which is why pundits were not surprised at all.

The formation of the UPC (Union of the Populations of the Camerouns) in French Cameroun in 1946 and the birth of sister union-nationalist (civic-nationalist) parties in British Cameroons highlighted the seriousness of the former Kamerunians to work together to build a "New Cameroon". By 1955, the UPC commanded more than 80% of popular support in French Cameroun.

So pundits considered it foolhardy when the French government issued a decree banning the UPC on July 13, 1955, in French Cameroons, a strategic act that was followed by the party's ban in British Cameroons three years later on the same fabricated charges of inciting violence and for being communists. These coordinated moves by Africa's two foremost colonial masters at the time were supposed to spell disaster for the dream held by Cameroon's leaders. Many Cameroonians saw nothing but duplicity and hypocrisy in the moves, wondering whether the freedom they had assisted the Free French Forces to achieve for France and its citizens was a special right or privilege meant for "White People" only.

When in 1956, the UPC resorted to a partisan war of liberation from French rule, it was a belated move to confront France after failing to resolve the ban in a peaceful manner. That war would end with the defeat of the UPC in 1970, a defeat that came with the assassinations and execution of the party's successive heads in 1958, 1960 and 1971, i.e., the deaths of Ruben Um Nyobe, Dr. Felix Moumie, and Ernest Ouandie respectively. It would leave Cameroon entrapped through a French-imposed system rooted in the Colonial Pact France made its puppets sign before allowing their countries to become members of the United Nations Organization by granting these former colonies string-controlled independence.

Despite the period of instability during the country's unsuccessful war of liberation that saw the French Trusteeship masters handing power to those who never asked for or never fought for it (the puppets that constitute the system today), despite the eventual peaceful reunification of British Southern Cameroons with the former French Cameroun, despite Cameroon's agricultural recovery and the discovery of oil in the 1970s that saw the country emerge as Africa's eight largest economy and the world's second fastest growing in the early 1980s, Cameroon is today in a horrible shape.

The Cameroonian economy that was expected to grow twenty times over the next thirty years, i.e., from 1982-2012, barely doubled over that period of time. Everything changed for the worse after Paul Biya was handed power in November 1982 by the first French-installed puppet Cameroonian president Ahmadou Ahidjo. Since then, Cameroon has experienced the biggest proportionate embezzlement of state funds ever recorded in Africa. And the country holds the sad record as the country in Africa that has experienced the worst peacetime impoverishment since 1960.

Today, president Paul Biya is presiding over a nation where more than 80% of its physicians are abroad, where more than 90% of its doctorate degree holders are abroad, where Cameroonians invest abroad more than at home, where Cameroonians are voting against the system with their feet; today, Cameroon's neighbors who before envied its high standards of living and saw it as a place of refuge and opportunities, now find Cameroonians envying them as they forge ahead with a sense of direction while Cameroon lags behind in its spiral towards total, complete and horrifying economic, social and political decay.

People unfamiliar with the Cameroonian situation would

be wondering why such an abysmal situation persists. Well; the answer is simple. Cameroon finds itself today in a situation like someone in a quicksand because of the anachronistic system put in place by Gaullist France when General Charles De Gaulle returned to power in 1958 and decided to make France's former colonies and territories members of the United Nations Organization (UNO), while controlling them with transparent or invisible strings this time. French Cameroun and British Southern Cameroons achieved independence and reunification all right, only for the people to find that the new country is quasi-independent under a broader French template of control variously described as FrancAfrique. This French-imposed system has traumatized, demoralized, divided and dehumanized the Cameroonian people over the years.

The Gaullist system put in place by the elites of the French political establishment has as one of its major objectives the exclusion from Cameroon's political power of the union-nationalists advocating for the reunification and independence of the divided territories of the former German Kamerun, civic nationalists who commanded the support of more than 80% of the populations of both territories of British Cameroons and French Cameroun in the 1950s and 1960s. The current system in Cameroon is a partnership of French imperial interest in Africa (economic and political) otherwise known as FrancAfrique and its Cameroonian collaborators (the renegades and anti-union-nationalists who never opposed and who do not object to France's neo-colonial stranglehold of Cameroon).

The system has been effective in infecting the minds of

many Cameroonians, reducing them into a state of hopelessness, in a process that lures them to direct their energy not against the Biya regime and the system, but at their neighbors. The system has successfully elevated corruption and the divide-and-rule strategy into an art—it has promoted the notion of settlers and indigenes, it has encouraged ethnocentrism, tribalism, clannishness, regional jingoism, sectarianism and other forms of division. We see a total and complete absence of strategic or even tactical planning when it comes to the economic and social development of the nation. We see a complete absence of social solidarity.

To compound the division and confusion among the people who reject the Biya regime and the French-imposed system, the so-called opposition leaders these freedom-craving Cameroonians had been looking up to have now been absorbed back into the system, leaving the struggling Cameroonian masses distrustful of politicians in general. Today, the down-trodden Cameroonian people are in a state of political lethargy.

When Paul Biya called for the holding of Senate elections in April 2013, eighteen years after his parliament promulgated a law to create one, most Cameroonians thought it would be another charade, as usual. It made no sense for the so-called opposition parties with a semblance of representation in parliament to glorify the charade with their participation. Most Cameroonians knew the system was sustaining these so-called opposition leaders financially and that some of them were in the government, but Cameroonians were not prepared for the extent to which these politicians would go to insult their intelligence. But deals between the ruling party and the opposition were made all right. The electoral masquerade took place and the people saw the ruling party campaigning for the so-called main opposition party (Social Democratic Front—SDF) in some regions of the country, while the SDF in the words of its chairman or president John Fru Ndi "...one good turn deserves another...", openly backed the ruling party, thereby ensuring its victory in other regions of the country.

How could that have happened? Politically-shocked Cameroonians have been asking themselves ever since the open fornication between the ruling party and the so-called opposition political parties in April 2013.

To prevent chaos and ensure a smooth succession, SDF spokes-persons, and apologists quip.

"Paul Biya has a deal with the SDF to hand over power to one of its members," some anonymous voices within the SDF echo.

If you ask me, my answer is clear. What was supposed to be a Cameroonian revolution that began on May 26, 1990, became a political comedy played by former members of the French-imposed system or political establishment, a political comedy that has gone full circle. The worldwide wind of change generated by Mikhail Gorbachev's Glasnost and Perestroika that swept away authoritarian systems in Eastern Europe and Africa, and that stirred the vast majority of Cameroonians in the 1990s to risk their lives in the streets demanding political change, was effectively controlled by the system. The desire for change that more than 80% of Cameroonians have has been hijacked by the authoritarian system in Cameroon and the so-called leaders of the opposition. The people got taken for a ride.

The biggest mistake made by Cameroonians was that when the clamor for change began, they followed Cameroonians who had no democratic credentials, people who hardly a year before, were in the upper echelons of power in the system, but who at the time claimed they had left the ruling party and now opposed it. All the so-called heads of what the world knows today as the prominent opposition parties in Cameroon (John Fru Ndi of the SDF, Bello Bouba Maigari of the UNDP, Ndam Njoya of the CDU etc.) were members of the ruling party right up to the year 1990, when the system was forced to accept multi-party politics in Cameroon. Like the Pied Piper, these so-called opposition leaders lured freedom-starved Cameroonians into greater despondence and political lethargy. Such a feat was achieved only because Cameroonian liberals, union-nationalists, revolutionaries, democrats and patriots who had always rejected the system, thought these so-called heads of the so-called new opposition, these people who were the first to make the moves to create political parties, shared the vision of the "New Cameroon" that Cameroonians fought, died and voted for, a vision that achieved the land's reunification and independence (though it has never been real because it got usurped by the evil system that today is under the leadership of Paul Biya and his French puppeteers.), but that is yet to realize democracy, freedom, liberalism, progress, justice, equality and development.

False are the statements by members of the compromised opposition that had they not openly embraced the Biya regime and the system, chaos would have ensued in Cameroon incase Biya exited the political scene. There is no truth in the statement because the system in Cameroon is authoritarian, not autocratic.

Authoritarian regimes are usually coated with a sublime idea that could be political (Stalinism/Marxism/Communism, Fascism etc.), that could be religious (Iranian and Taliban theocracy etc.) or that could be an interest arrangement (FrancAfrique). in Cameroon, the system is built around preventing those who believe in the Cameroonian struggle (the union-nationalists, otherwise called the Kamerunists) from attaining power.

The system in Cameroon is a collection of individual interest groups, bringing together the propagators of French neo-colonialism and their Cameroonian collaborators. Paul Biya is the head of the collaborationists. And in many ways, he has been acting over the years as an absentee president. Meanwhile, the state has been functioning zombie-like during his quasi-presence. As a matter of fact, even though the mortifying arrangement suited the interest of the puppeteers and the beneficiaries of the system, it exposed the system to popular uprisings since that means the beneficiaries of the system are not clearly or functionally organized. With the advent of social media, globalization, the maturity of post-independence generations that never benefited from the system; and with the soldiers of the 1990s phase of the struggle dissociating themselves from the so-called opposition leaders, the authoritarian system now finds itself even more vulnerable.

The authoritarian system would be faced by a new political force that never associated itself with the system, a new political force that embodies the spirit of the century-old struggle for the "NEW KAMERUN" or "NEW CAMEROON" that confronted German colonial control, stood up to French duplicity in the land in a war that decimated more than half a million of its supporters; the authoritarian system would be faced by a new force that embraces the legacy of those who fought, died and voted for the independence and reunification of Cameroon, a new force that rejects all the values of the system that the French political mafia over Africa put in place in their game plan to control the destiny of Cameroon, a six-decade-old evil system that can only lead the country to abyss.

Now, as the open and hidden collaborators of the system openly embrace one another (the ruling party and the so-called heads of the so-called opposition parties) starting with the recent senatorial charade where the so-called principal opposition—the Social Democratic Front (SDF) and the party of Paul Biya—Cameroon People's Democratic Movement (CPDM) supported each other's aspirations in agreed-upon provinces with guaranteed votes from party members, the system is encouraging the creation of elite groups of beneficiaries who see or think that their political and economic survival rests only in a continuation or sustenance of the system. We are observing the evolvement of a system that is shedding any pretense of limited political pluralism; we are observing the entrenchment of a system that openly views the people as its number one enemy. Such a system then becomes autocratic.

In a nutshell, Cameroon's so-called opposition political parties that are in symbiosis with the authoritarian system are aiding the system in its gradual transition into an autocratic system, thereby ensuring its survival in a morphed form. The rapidly changing system needs a strong man to be truly autocratic. This would be someone who has hands on the job to act as the president, someone who the French puppeteers would like to portray as the benevolent despot.

As Egyptian writer Alaa Al -Aswany said, "The concept of the benevolent dictator, just like the concepts of the noble thief or the honest whore, is no more than a meaningless fantasy."

It is the place of post-independence Cameroonians to reject whatever farce the system comes up with as change whenever power passes down to the generation after Paul Biya. By absorbing former members of his party who for decades identified with the opposition, Biya is trying to give Cameroonians and the rest of the world the impression that Cameroon's opposition is in sync with his vision for the political evolution of Cameroon. Unfortunately, the system does not intend to let the majority of Cameroonians participate or have a say in Cameroon's political development or evolution.

The New Cameroon will be founded. Not by beneficiaries of the system (past and present) but by those who have always rejected it as an evil system that has been leading Cameroon into the abyss.

But then, in founding the New Cameroon, patriotic, honest, democratic, unbiased and progressive-minded Cameroonians would have to reconcile a country where:

- the system made sure that most of its historic figures who dedicated their lives and even died for the cause for Cameroon's reunification and independence got killed and buried like dogs at home and abroad,
- the bodies of some of these historic figures that got buried abroad are missing,
- a few of the historic figures who thought they could contribute in nation-building got sidelined, cowed and humiliated by the system,
- its first head of state died and is buried abroad,
- and where the people have been insulted for more than five decades by the regimes of Ahmadou Ahidjo and Paul Biya through an imposed minority system that sowed the seeds of division, corruption, mediocrity, fear, and despondency that are haunting Cameroon today.

The ideas and ideals of the New Cameroon hatched by the country's historic civic-nationalists and developed over the years by post-independence union-nationalists is Cameroon's only bargain with the future. It is the only nucleus around which Cameroon can reconcile with its turbulent past; it is the nucleus that all the strata of Cameroonian society can connect to in the process of nation-building; it is the only nucleus around which a free, democratic, liberal, fair and prosperous Cameroon can be built. The New Cameroon would lead the country in taking its merited place in the central African region, Africa as a whole, and the world at large. That would be possible only if we confine the legacies of the Ahidjo/Biya regimes and the suffocating French-imposed system to the dustbin of history.

Janvier Tchouteu   *06/04/2013*

Chapter Six

Quotes

I will never forget the moment when, for the first time, I felt and understood the tragedy of colonization. [. ..] Since that day, I am ashamed of my country. Since that day, I cannot meet an Indochinese, an Algerian, a Moroccan, without wanting to ask for forgiveness. Forgive all the pains, all the humiliations that have been made to suffer, that we made their people suffer. Because their oppressor is the French state, that does it in the name of all the French, therefore also, for a small part, in my name. That is why, in the presence of those whom the French State oppresses, I cannot but blush, I cannot but feel that I have faults to redeem myself of.

- Simone Weil

Between colonizer and colonized, there is room only for chore, intimidation, pressure, police, robbery, rape, compulsory cultures, contempt, mistrust, arrogance, sufficiency, Whistling, decrepit elites, degraded masses. No human contact, but relations of domination and submission that transform the colonizing man into a pawn, adjutant, babysitter, chicote; and the native man into an instrument of production. It's my turn to ask an equation: colonization = change.

- Aimé Césaire

Neocolonialism is nothing but a slow and progressive destruction of the emancipation of peoples.
-Souleymane Boel

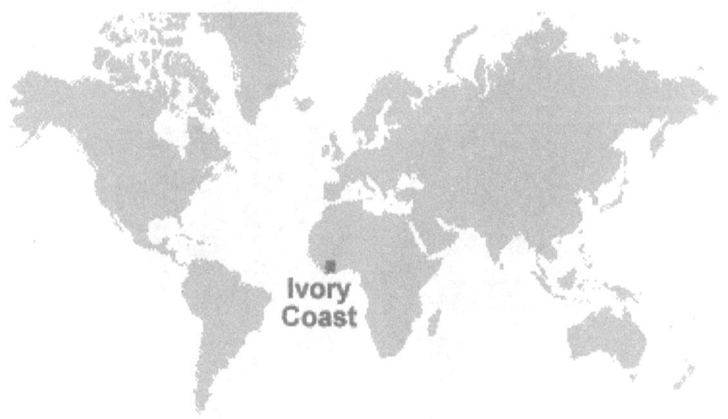

From Left to Right: Laurent Gbagbo and Alassane Ouattara

Often times, the most complicated peace is better than the simplest war. Both Laurent Gbagbo and Alassane Ouattara are losers and both led the Ivorian people towards a losing path. I pity them both, because I think there is a nucleus of goodness in their souls when it comes to their desires and their overall commitment to the wellbeing of Cote D'Ivoire.

There are tons of lessons to learn from the decade old Ivorian quagmire that ultimately led to the humiliation of a naïve Gbagbo and the crippled ascension to power of Ouattara; one of which is that the arena of African power play or politics is a battle ground of ancient Greek classic proportions, like "The Iliad", where the warriors reel in their bravado, unconscious of the external influences of the greater powers (the gods) in their victories, defeats, survivals or escapes. The 1990s *Parlement generation* of Cameroon, especially those of the later years, suffer deeply from that incomprehension, which among other reasons is why the anachronistic French-imposed system is surviving in Cameroon. It is also why the absentee Paul Biya, the French puppet who has been passing around for thirty-six years as the president of Cameroon easily pulls off masquerades of fake elections that his Western puppet-masters validate by recognizing the false results of these elections.

It becomes obvious from the debacle between Gbagbo and Ouattara that the source of the rift between the two comes from the system imposed by France and their degree of acceptance or allegiance to this system that safeguards France's interest in the country, even above that of Ivory Coast. This French-imposed system makes Quattara a benevolent mercenary overseeing the management of Ivory Coast and casts Gbagbo as someone who was initially coerced but managed to overcome his inferiority complex into becoming a recalcitrant renegade.

France's detrimental involvement in African local politics especially after it pushed these countries into civil conflicts has been done with impunity, usually masqueraded as French efforts to save lives in areas they controlled in the past and ensured peace and prosperity during their colonial rule. In a nutshell, France and the squabbling successors of Félix Houphouët-Boigny (Konan Bedie, Ouattara, and General Gei etc) saw Gbagbo's 2000 electoral victory as an unacceptable mistake on their part that needed correction. Developments in the country after that, whether directly or indirectly, stemmed from that conception.

Countries like Cameroon will never be free unless France accepts the error of its ways one way or the other. And some Africans are not helping the process of growth, the procedures involved in France taking itself out of its entrapment vis-à-vis its loop-sided relationship with its former colonies and territories in Africa where even though France is viewed internationally, especially among the community of advanced nations as a law-abiding, civilizing and progressive nation, it has been carrying on in its relations with these Francophone nations in a mafia-like manner or like a dehumanized mafia don operating in a clandestine manner and acting with impunity.

In a nutshell, France's behavior in these African countries is like that of someone who is unconcerned about the welfare of the African people. In fact, it is hard to argue against some pundits who believe that it is outright racist and that it feeds on the minds of bigots who hold the twisted view of the child-like innocence or ignorance of the African, and who revel in the delusionary perception of Africans as a people incapable of coming up with anything good.

We would be hard-pressed to find someone with a strong enough argument that it is not a good idea to dismantle the political and economic system France implanted in its former colonies in Africa in the 1960s before granting them independence, thereby nurturing political establishments in those new African countries that look out for France interests there than the interests of these new nation-states. Such a process of knocking down the anachronistic system in the different African countries, which in their totality constitutes FrancAfrique, is a process that can be accomplished only by genuine civic-nationalists with the revolutionary drive, pan-Africanist vision and a deep love for their people. That is why advocates of the New Africa should be chided when they come out blindly against those Africans who in their amateurish and short-sighted ways confronted the full machinery of the conspiratorial powers (or god-like powers when analogizing from ancient Greek mythology).

I won't comment deeply on this Ivorian problem. We will face it again in Cameroon; and the rest of Central Africa will be gripped by similar deceptions in the next couple of years. But one thing for sure is that this French pattern has been in application for close to a century in Africa, which is why those in the French political establishment managing the political and economic control of Africa, the system of control of Francophone Africa

(FrancAfrique) view FrancAfrique as a successful template been a winning strategy, that does not require changing.

The job of the post-independence advocates of change is to study the methods of of control employed by foreign powers that are keeping Africans under perpetual helplessness and chaos to the point where the organizers of the chaos end up looking like the saviors. Africans should understand their history, master the levers of power and know that their salvation rests only in them sticking together and accepting one another as indispensable contributors to a future, prosperous and free country and continent.

I say so with sadness because two days ago, I talked with ex-Zairois who blamed Lumumba for the deplorable state of The Democratic Republic of Congo today, accusing him of taking Congo to independence when they were not ready, of bringing Mobuto to power and for not sharing his vision with the other politicians. It is like blaming Jesus Christ for his betrayal by Judas. And Congo, the sick heart of Africa will find itself trapped for eternity in incomprehension if it does not reconcile itself to its paralyzing history inflicted on the infant nation by the powers that plotted Lumumba's ouster and death.

Equally, in a three-way discourse with a Dutch professor in Amsterdam in 2003, a fellow compatriot argued forcefully that there has never been a war in Cameroon, that no massacres were carried out by French and Ahidjo forces, that Biya is a great leader and that Cameroon was doing great, which is why it is better off than most African countries. A fool's paradise I called it. Or was he gripped by the *Potemkin syndrome* at the time? Not until the young man read Triple Agent, Double Cross afterward, not until after he had his curiosity aroused and not until after he did some research of his own, did he lament the degree of brainwashing he and most Cameroonians had been subjected to. He was still suffering the effects of the brainwashing he underwent in Cameroon, even while studying and living in Europe's most liberal country.

Africans need to emancipate themselves from the mental slavery that still has most of Africa trapped in incomprehension and suffering from a lack of sense of direction. The lucky ones, especially those in the Diaspora, should be leading the effort of emancipation.

April 13, 2011   *Janvier Tchouteu*

Chapter Seven

Patrice Lumumba

Patrice Lumumba Quotes

"The colonialists care nothing for Africa for her own sake. They are attracted by African riches and their actions are guided by the desire to preserve their interests in Africa against the wishes of the African people. For the colonialists all means are good if they help them to possess these riches."

"The day will come when history will speak. But it will not be the history which will be taught in Brussels, Paris, Washington or the United Nations...Africa will write its own history and in both north and south, it will be a history of glory and dignity."

"Political independence has no meaning if it is not accompanied by rapid economic and social development."

"Without dignity there is no liberty, without justice there is no dignity, and without independence there are no free men."

"A minimum of comfort is necessary for the practice of virtue."

"The only thing which we wanted for our country is the right to a worthy life, to dignity without pretense, to independence without restrictions. This was never the desire of the Belgian colonialists and their Western allies..."

"These divisions, which the colonial powers have always exploited the better to dominate us, have played an important role—and are still playing that role—in the suicide of Africa."

"We know that Africa is neither French, nor British, nor

American, nor Russian, that it is African. We know the objects of the West. Yesterday they divided us on the level of a tribe, clan and village…They want to create antagonistic blocs, satellites…"

"No one is perfect in this imperfect world."

"African unity and solidarity are no longer dreams. They must be expressed in decisions."

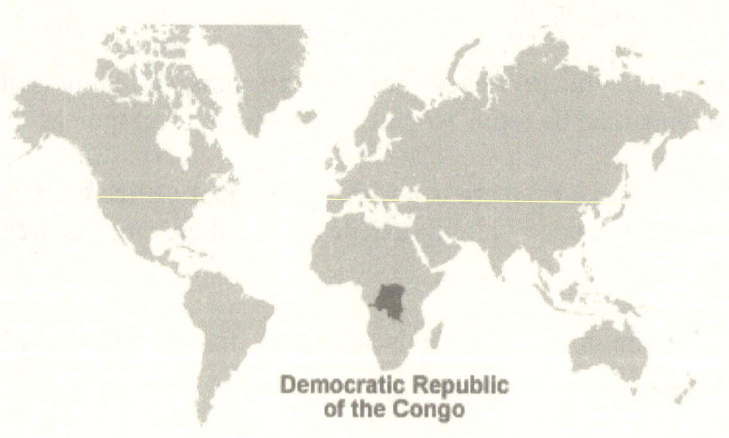

Patrice Lumumba shortly before his death

The January 17, 1961 assassination of Patrice Lumumba, the first democratically elected prime minister of what is today the Democratic Republic of the Congo (DRC), is considered by many Africans as "the most important assassination of the 20th century" because it not only wrecked the country, but it also polarized and paralyzed Africa, resulting in a disunity that the continent has yet to recover from. This heinous crime was a culmination of two inter-related assassination plots by elements within the American and Belgian governments that made use of Congolese accomplices and a Belgian execution squad to carry out the slaying of the leader of this infant nation in the heart of Africa that just got its independence from Belgium on 30 June 1960.

Historians, sociologists and geo-political pundits all agree that Congo is the most traumatized country in Africa and the world, and that of all the atrocities that Congo experienced in its abused history, Patrice Lumumba's assassination was the single cruelest act. In fact, it is rightly viewed as the country's original sin.

The assassination took place less than seven months after the independence of this territory occupying 7. 7% of the landmass of Africa. The act transformed into a stumbling block to the hopes of implementing the lofty ideals of Congolese national unity, material prosperity, democracy, economic independence, liberty and pan-African solidarity that Lumumba had been championing. What cannot be overlooked in particular is the fact that his assassination served as a shattering blow to the hopes, dreams and aspirations of millions of Congolese, and it disillusioned an even greater number of Africans across the continent.

The fact that one of the Soviet Union's largest universities—The Peoples' Friendship University of Russia—that was founded on February 05, 1960 got renamed "The Patrice Lumumba University" on February 22, 1961, and the fact that this institution of higher learning went on to educate close to a hundred thousand foreigners, most of them Africans, highlights the historical significance of the young African's death to Africa and the rest of the world during the Cold War.

As it turns out, the assassination's historical importance

lies in a multitude of factors, of which the most relevant at the time were based on the global context in which it took place (President Eisenhower authorized the assassination and the CIA carried out his abduction and transfer; the United Nations, its Secretary General Dag Hammarskjöld, the Soviet Union and the British M16 were involved in the debacle; and the Belgians directed his murder and those of his two associates before later getting rid of the bodies by digging them up and dissolving them in sulfuric acid, and then grounding and scattering the bones), its impact on Congolese politics since then, and Lumumba's overall legacy as a civic-nationalist leader and pan-Africanist icon. After all, he was working with Félix Moumié, the Cameroonian liberation movement leader that the French Secret Service (SDECE) poisoned in Geneva, Switzerland on 3 November 1960.

One question that has been prevalent in the geopolitical sphere is this:

Why did the USA, Britain, France and Belgium get involved in the assassination of Congo's first democratically elected leader?

It all began in April 1884, seven months before the Berlin Congress, when the United States of America became the first country in the world to recognize the claims of the Belgian King Leopold II to the territories of the Congo Basin. These territories became known as the Congo Free State. King Leopold ruled it as his private property, making use of a small cadre of white administrators that were drawn from across Europe.

The Congo Free State made King Leopold one of the wealthiest monarchs in the world, an outsized accomplishment given the fact that he was the king of Belgium, which was such a small country in the neighborhood of mighty geopolitical entities like the British, German, Russian and Austro-Hungarian Empires. But the Belgian king's wealth was accumulated at an enormous cost to the native African population who were forced to provide unpaid labor that was not different from slavery, in the exploitation of the land's mineral, forest and agricultural resources for the Belgian monarch. However, when the atrocities related to the brutal economic exploitation in King Leopold's Congo Free State resulted in millions of fatalities, the United States of America joined other world powers and forced the Belgian state to take over the Congo Free State as a regular colony and stop the killings and maiming of the native Congolese population— a genocide per se.

It was only after Congo got transformed into a regular colony that the United States of America acquired a strategic stake in the enormous natural wealth of the territory. In fact, the USA used the uranium from Congolese mines to manufacture the first atomic weapons that were used on the Japanese cities of Hiroshima and Nagasaki, leading to an abrupt end of the Second World War in the Pacific.

The strategic importance of resources-rich Congo in particular, and resources-rich Africa in general, especially in helping the Allies win the Second World War, became a curse afterwards when the continent sought independence from its colonial masters. This was at a time that the Cold War was dominating geopolitics. America and its Western allies resolved to give the colonies independence all right, but not the type of independence the rest of the world knew about. The Western powers were not prepared to let the people of the African colonies have effective control over the strategic raw materials in their territories, for fear that these assets could fall into the hands of the countries of the Soviet or communist camp. That was why western interests perceived a threat in Patrice Lumumba's resolve to achieve genuine independence for Congo and to gain full control over country's resources for use in developing the infant nation and in improving the living conditions of the Congolese people.

To stop Patrice Lumumba, the United States of America and Belgium left no stone unturned, including the use of the United Nations secretariat under Dag Hammarskjöld and Ralph Bunche, the buying of the support of Lumumba's Congolese rivals, the silencing of some African leaders supportive of Lumumba and the pan-Africanist goal he shared, and the buying of the services of killers for hire (mercenaries) to eliminate the obstacle to their smooth control of Congo, a country they intended to be nothing more than a quasi-independent state subservient to the western leaders and western interests.

Right after granting independence to Congo on June 30, 1960, Belgium and its western allies went about undermining the infant nation's stability by encouraging a virulent opposition to Lumumba's government, using western-backed Congolese politicians. In fact, by December 1960, Congo was effectively under four separate governments, three of which were under the thumbs of the anti-Lumumba factions backed by Western Powers. These were:

- the central government in the Congolese capital of Léopoldville (Kinshasa)
- a rival central government established by Lumumba's followers in Stanleyville (Kisangani)
- a secessionist regime in the mineral-rich province of Katanga under the leadership of Moise Tshombe
- and another secessionist administration in the South Kasai province under the leadership of Albert Kalonji.

With Lumumba liquidated half a year after the granting of independence to Congo, with the removal of what the Western geopolitical players perceived as the major threat to their interests in the new country, Belgium, Britain, France and the United States of America led international efforts to spread the authority of the moderate and pro-western regime in Kinshasa over the entire Congo. It was a two-pronged strategy involving the use of the new Western-created Congolese army under the command of the Western-backed regime of Mobutu Sese Seko, and the use of United Nations peacekeepers. The strategy was so effective that the Lumumbist stronghold in the East of the country centered around Kisangani, fell in August 1961. South Kasai folded in September 1962, and the Katanga secession was reversed in January 1963.

After wrecking the newly independent Congo to undermine Lumumba, after assassinating Lumumba and installing a puppet government, and then directing it in bringing the country together again, the Western powers were surprised when a radical social movement for a "second independence" arose, challenging the neocolonial state and its pro-western leadership. It was a mass movement of workers, lower civil servants, the urban unemployed, peasants and students. They were provided leadership by Lumumba's lieutenants, most of whom had regrouped in the former French Congolese capital of Brazzaville, across the Congo river from the former Belgian Congolese capital city of Kinshasa. In October 1963, these Lumumbists established a National Liberation Council (CNL) with a mission to oust the Mobutu regime and create a New Congo. They were taken seriously to the point where the Soviet Union gave them military assistance. Some of the few surviving pan-Africanist governments in the continent provided support as well. Even Ernesto Che Guevara, the Argentine revolutionary icon and Fidel Castro's second in command, set up base in Congo to help them. In fact, when Che Guevara wrote in 1964 that:

"We must move forward, striking out tirelessly against imperialism. From all over the world, we have to learn lessons which events afford. Lumumba's murder should be

a lesson for all of us."

He began the immortalization of Patrice Lumumba after failing in his Congo expedition to galvanize the Lumumbists against the Western puppet government of Mobutu Sese Seko.

In all the continents of the world today, streets, parks, squares, airports, statues and other infrastructures abound that bear the name Lumumba in honor of an altruist, a man who embraced union-nationalism, opposed the division of his country along ethnic or regional lines, and who supported pan-Africanism and the liberation of all the colonial territories not only in Africa, but also in the rest of the world.

Patrice Lumumba's legacy continues to serve as an inspiration in Congolese politics today, as dozens of political parties proclaim their belief in his ideas of "Positive Neutralism," which advocates a return to African values and which rejects any imported ideology, including that of the Soviet Union:

"We are not Communists or Catholics. We are African nationalists," Patrice Lumumba once said.

Pan-Africanists (those who dream of a future African Economic Union with an integrated political system and military structure) cherish the Lumumba legacy and place him alongside Nkwame Nkrumah of Ghana, Sekou Touré of Guinea, Julius Nyerere of Tanzania and the liquidated leaders of Cameroon's historic UPC party that led the fight for the country's unification and independence, as the icons of the independence era that sowed the seeds for the yet to be realized African Union.

Chapter Eight

Anwar al-Sadat

Anwar al-Sadat Quotes

"Peace is much more precious than a piece of land... let there be no more wars."

"He who cannot change the very fabric of his thought will never be able to change reality."

"There can be hope only for a society which acts as one big family, not as many separate ones."

"Most people seek after what they do not possess and are enslaved by the very things they want to acquire."

"Fear is, I believe, a most effective tool in destroying the soul of an individual - and the soul of a people."

"Great suffering has a silver-lining that we can be grateful for, because it builds up a human being and puts him or her within reach of self-knowledge."

"This [fundamentalism] is not religion. It is obscenity. These are lies, the criminal use of religious power to misguide people."

"There is no happiness for people at the expense of other people."

"I believe that for peace a man may, even should, do everything in his power. Nothing in this world could rank higher than peace."

"If you don't have the capacity to change yourself and your own attitudes, then nothing around you can be changed."

"Fear is, I believe, a most effective tool in destroying the soul of an individual - and the soul of a people."

"Russians can give you arms but only the United States can give you a solution."

"I do not care for socially recognizable success. I only value that success which I can feel within me, which satisfies me, and which basically stems from self-knowledge."

"To love means to give, and to give means to build, while to hate is to destroy."

"I was brought up to believe that how I saw myself was more important than how others saw me."

"There can be hope only for a society which acts as one big family, not as many separate ones."

"Let there be no more war or bloodshed between Arabs and Israelis. Let there be no more suffering or denial of rights. Let there be no more despair or loss of faith."

"Real success is success with self. It's not in having things, but in having mastery, having victory over self."

"Faith means that a man should regard any disaster simply as a fate-determined blow which must be endured."

"I was brought up to believe that how I saw myself was more important than how others saw me."

"Only when he has ceased to need things can a man truly be his own master and so really exist."

"There is no happiness for people at the expense of other people."

"Land is immortal, for it harbors the mysteries of creation."

"Let every girl, let every woman, let every mother here [in Israel]-and there in my country [Egypt]-know we shall solve all our problems through negotiations around the table rather than starting war."

Anwar al-Sadat was born in Upper Egypt on December 25, 1918, into a family of 13 children, and grew up 40 miles north of Cairo at a time that Egypt was a British protectorate. The status of Egypt under the control of the British Empire came about from the crippling debt that forced the Egyptian government to sell its interests in the French engineered Suez Canal to the British government.

Constructed between 1859 and 1869, the Suez Canal is an artificial sea-level waterway in Egypt that connects the Mediterranean Sea to the Red Sea through the Isthmus of Suez. The canal offers watercrafts a shorter journey between the North Atlantic and northern Indian Ocean, thereby reducing the journey by approximately 7, 000 kilometers (4, 300 miles). In fact, the British and the French had been using the resources of the canal to establish enough political control over Egypt that it was logical to refer to Egypt as a British colony.

Sadat would be greatly affected by four figures in his early life—Zahran from Sadat's home village who was hanged by the British for a riot that resulted in the death of a British officer; Kemal Ataturk who created the modern state of Turkey from the ashes of the Ottoman Empire; Mohandas (Mahatma) Gandhi who had preached the power of nonviolence in combating injustice while touring Egypt in 1932; and finally Adolf Hitler whom Sadat viewed as someone who could help unshackle Egypt from British colonial control.

When the British created a military school in Egypt in 1936 following an agreement with the Egyptian Wafd party, Sadat became one of its first students. After his graduation, the government posted him to Sudan where he met Gamal Abdel Nasser, with whom, along with several other junior officers, he formed the secret Free Officers, a movement dedicated to revolution that would free Egypt and Sudan from the domination of the British and the corruption of the monarchy. This political association would eventually lead them to the Egyptian presidency.

Sadat would be jailed twice for his revolutionary activities during The Second World War. This was precisely for his efforts to obtain help from the Axis Powers (Italy and Germany) to expel the British. After his release from prison, he reconnected with Nasser only to find out that their movement had grown considerably during the years that he was under incarceration. On July 23, 1952, the Free Officers Organization overthrew King Farouk and brought an end to the Egyptian monarchy in a military coup d'état that launched the Egyptian Revolution of 1952. Thereafter, he became Nasser's public relations minister and trusted lieutenant. The hardworking and focused Sadat would accomplish Nasser's order to oversee the official abdication of King Farouk.

It was during Nasser's years in power that Sadat learned the dangerous game of nation-building in a world of superpower rivalries. They led Egypt into becoming a "non-aligned" country, hence one of the leading nations that underdeveloped and post-colonial societies looked up to. Nasser and Sadat would survive the 1956 war after Nasser nationalized the Suez Canal, prompting the British, the French, and the Israelis to launch an attack on Egypt in a bid to wrestle control of the canal from Egyptian hands. The 1956 war would only end after the United States of America forced Britain, France and Israel to withdraw their forces from Egypt. The two comrades tapped the war to the point that Egypt emerged from that war as a champion of the non-aligned countries for resisting the big powers.

Nasser's prominence would take a beating from the debacle of the 1967 Six-Day War when the Israeli military completely destroyed the Egyptian air forces and incapacitated the Egyptian Army by killing at least 3, 000 soldiers and occupying the Sinai Peninsula all the way to the Suez Canal. The outcome of the war put a strain on the Egyptian economy and almost bankrupted the government. What was even more disheartening for Nasser was the growing disunity among the squabbling Arab nations and the growing Palestinian movements. His death on September 29, 1970, from a heart attack, came about from his declining health caused by Egypt's defeat in the 1967 Arab-Israeli war.

Called "Nasser's black poodle" by some Egyptians of high ranking, Sadat was underrated when he succeeded Nasser. However, he proved himself over the next 11 years to be an astute leader of his people. When he openly offered the Israelis a peace treaty in exchange for the Sinai Peninsula captured by Israel in the 1967 war, many, especially in the Arab world, were taken aback. Still, he would surmount the domestic crisis and international intrigues that plagued his presidency. He would make the Soviet Union take him seriously by expelling them after they failed to replenish Egypt's depleted military supplies, and then repairing relations with them again.

When on October 6, 1973, Sadat attacked Israel in a bid to recapture the Sinai Peninsula after the Jewish state continued to refuse the Egyptian peace initiative, it was his biggest military and political gamble. It almost paid off since excellent military precision enabled the Egyptian army to cross the Suez Canal back into the Sinai where they began driving the Israeli army into the desert. Even though the successes during the war were short-lived and much of the gains of the Egyptian Army were reversed, the attack created a new momentum for peace in Egypt and in Israel, as both states came out of the war war-weary, with battered economies and a sense of how close they were to doom. However, the war raised the attention and concerns of the international community, especially the United States of America that feared greater instability in the Middle East and North Africa.

Sadat came out of the war convinced that peace with Israel would reap an enormous "peace dividend," and so initiated his most important diplomatic gamble by affirming in a speech to the Egyptian parliament in 1977, that he would go anywhere to negotiate a peace agreement with the Israelis, even to the Israeli parliament. The Israelis took him at his words with an invitation to do just that— address the Israeli parliament known as the Knesset, something he did, thereby initiating a new momentum for peace that would eventually culminate in the 1978 Camp David Accords and Egypt and Israel signing a final peace treaty in 1979. He and the Israeli Prime Minister Menachem Begin would win the Nobel Prize for Peace that year for their efforts in realizing peace between their two states.

Even though the peace treaty with Israel made it possible for Egypt to get the Sinai back and even though it provides the country assistance from the West, assistance that has been helping the Egyptian economy recover and even prosper, it left Egypt shunned by the rest of the Arab world. Sadat's coziness with the West and the peace treaty with Israel also stirred up a great deal of domestic opposition, especially among the country's fundamentalist Muslim groups. Even though he improved the everyday life of the common Egyptian, even though he made Sharia the basis of all new Egyptian laws, and even though he sought to restore calm to the nation by enacting laws outlawing protest, Muslim fundamentalist would not be satisfied.

It was that dissatisfaction that led to the assassination of Sadat on October 6, 1981, during a military parade celebrating the successful Suez crossing by the Egyptian Army during the 1973 War against Israel. His vice President, Hosni Mubarak would succeed him.

Three US. Presidents—Gerald Ford, Jimmy Carter and Richard Nixon would attend Sadat's funeral. The only Arab head of state to pay his last honor to the assassinated Egyptian leader was Gaafar Nimeiry of Sudan, a move that would cost him dearly as he would be overthrown by Islamists on April 6, 1985.

Even though Sadat's bold step in making peace with Israel cost him his life and led to Egypt's expulsion from the Arab League, it opened the door for future negotiations between Israel and the rest of the Arab world, making it possible for the Oslo Accords between Israel and the Palestinian Liberation Organization (PLO) that was signed in 1993. The signing of the peace treaty between Israel and Jordan in 1994, making Jordan the second Arab country to conclude peace with Israel, owes a lot to the pioneering peace Sadat led Egypt to sign with Israel. Today, Israel has developed non-diplomatic ties with several other Arab countries, and is recognized by several Muslim countries.

Sadat is honored in Malaysia where he is an Honorary Grand Commander of the Order of the Defender of the Realm.

Today, close to four decades after his death, Anwar Sadat, if you ask Egyptians who knew him, experienced his rule or learned about his life and death, you are likely to get a mixed ranged of reactions. However, the emotions you will see on their faces the most are those reflecting respect, gratitude and pain. Most secular Egyptians embrace his legacy, holding that he was daring leader, a visionary, a realist, a pragmatist, a humane person and a genuine patriot unencumbered by the idealism. However, most of those who think he left behind a negative legacy, think he betrayed the Arab cause by making a separate peace with Israel, which only promises more violence in the future, and that the prosperity he promised would follow the signing of the Egyptian-Israeli peace treaty at Camp David in the USA was overhyped. As a matter of fact there are other Egyptians who go as far as attacking the fundamentals of his character, claiming that he was frequently deceitful, vain and indolent, and that he even acted the buffoon every now and then, especially to his superiors.

While most pundits agree that Sadat's predecessor Gamal Abdul Nasser put the bricks together for the foundation of the modern Egyptian state, another popular view is that Sadat completed the foundation of modern Egypt and shaped the country's internal and external development---socio-economic and political in a very fundamental way, setting Egypt on a trajectory that hardly any other leader or political movement can sway it away from. And he did so at a time that most Arab regimes had fallen into "moral and political degeneracy, thereby freeing Egypt from their bankrupt policies.

Sadat's critics, especially the harshest ones like the Islamists (the Muslim Brotherhood in particular) that he repressed, hold him responsible for making it difficult for democracy to grow in Egypt. Some of them even consider him an incompetent administrator who made a mockery of the law in repressing his real or imagined opponents, and who fostered corruption among his inner and outer circle.

No matter what position a critique of Sadat takes, one thing that cannot be disputed is the fact that he inherited an Egypt from Gamal Abdul Nasser that was partially occupied by Israel, defeated, bankrupt, heavily on the Soviet Union; and he left it a country that is more vibrant and secure.

Chapter Nine

Libya on a map of the world

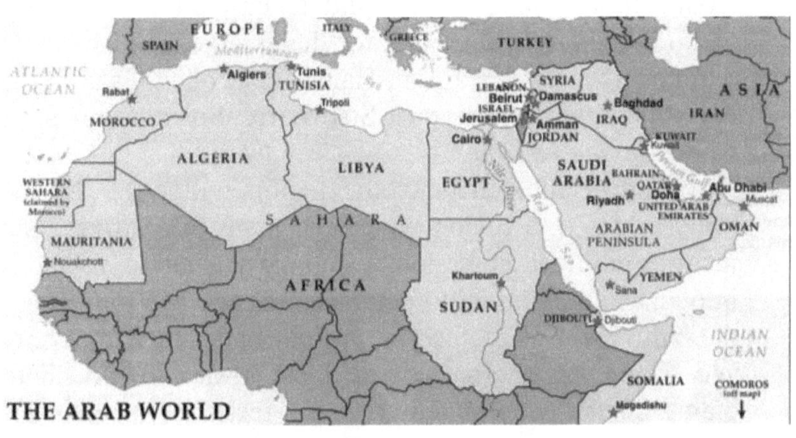

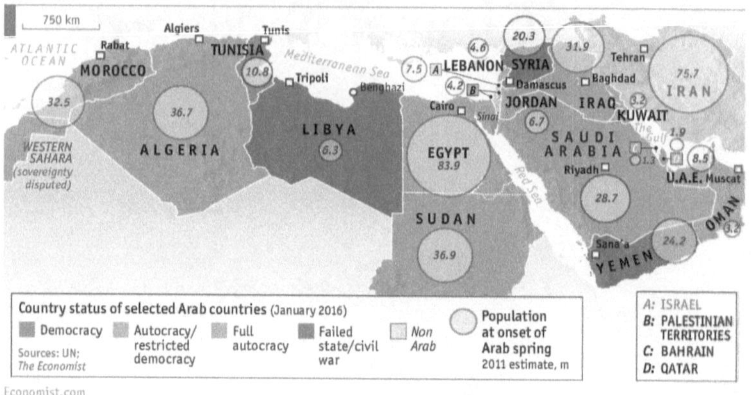

The Arab Spring

As the world watches the manifestation of "People's Power" (PP) in the Greater Middle East, the question that dominates is—How far would it go? Would it be like Eastern Europe between 1989-1990 when undemocratic leftist regimes were brought down, ushering in a new era of freedom, reforms, economic liberalization, liberal democracy and integration with the rest of Europe; or would the rumblings in the Middle East produce anarchy and provide a fertile ground for the emergence of barbaric regimes like post-shah Iran, Hamas-controlled Gaza in the Palestinian territories, post-Siad-Barre Somalia or post-Najibulla Afghanistan?

Whatever the outcome, the region will never be the same again. In a region where the myth of a strong man justifies political repression, economic stagnation, religious intolerance, the failure to embrace progress and modernity, the cultivation of myths that are out of touch with reality and where an external enemy must always be found to blame for the peoples' miseries, the feet and voices in the streets come as a welcome relief.

Whether we like it or not, the chaos in the streets is producing positive change that the dictatorial Islamists, pro-Western regimes and anti-western regimes cannot stop. The peoples' voices will never be taken for granted again. It is against this backdrop that The Muslim Brotherhood is shy about advocating a radical agenda of seizing power for itself in Egypt and why fundamentalists were left in the cold in Tunisia.

Never again would a dictator impose himself on the Tunisian people for more than a decade. Never would an absolute monarchy in Morocco deny the people their basic rights and freedom, and never again would presidents impose their sons on their nations as successors after their deaths. That means Assad would have to leave either honorably or otherwise. The mullahs in Iran would have to give power back to the people or lose their people and give their interpretation of the religion a bad name. The Gulf States would have to implement social and political reforms to match their economic progress. And even Saudi Arabia would have to stop treating its people like clueless children. The other Maghreb states and the rest of the region need to move with the positive wing of change or else find themselves swept by it.

It is against the backdrop of a progressive and tolerant Middle East emerging from the current uncertainty that the Big Powers should revise their policies on treating other dictatorships in the rest of the world. Corrupt anti-people dictatorships abound in Africa. Paul Biya of Cameroon otherwise known as the crafter of the best election-rigging machinery in the world has been in power for twenty nine years, supported in his stay by his French masters. He would practice his election-rigging art again in October of 2011. Others like him thrive in central, west and southern Africa. Only with the dismantling of these regimes will there be economic and democratic progress in these regions.

Strong voices are emerging to facilitate this process of democratization. The progressive world should not fail to take sides with these advocates of change, these propagators of democracy and freedom when the moment arrives. They are the African continent's only bargain with the future.

February 9, 2011

Janvier T. Chando is an author and political writer.

Chapter Ten

Muammar al-Qaddafi

MUAMMAR GADDAFI QUOTES

"Nations whose nationalism is destroyed are subject to ruin."

"Man's freedom is lacking if somebody else controls what he needs, for need may result in man's enslavement of man."

"Let the free people of the world know that we could have bargained over and sold out our cause in return for a personal secure and stable life. We received many offers to this effect, but we chose to be at the vanguard of the confrontation as a badge of duty and honor."

"I have nothing but scorn for the notion of an Islamic bomb. There is no such thing as an Islamic bomb or a Christian bomb. Any such weapon is a means of terrorizing humanity, and we are against the manufacture and acquisition of nuclear weapons. This is in line with our definition of-and opposition to-terrorism."

"I won't be a party to a conspiracy to mobilize the Arabs against the Persians. Only the forces of colonialism benefit from such a conspiracy. I won't be a party to a conspiracy that splits Islam into two - Shiite Islam and Sunni Islam - mobilizing Sunni Islam against Shiite Islam."

"The times of Arab nationalism and unity are gone forever. These ideas which mobilized the masses are only a worthless currency. Libya has had to put up with too much from the Arabs for whom it has poured forth both blood and money."

For a little while longer, the story of Muammar al-Qaddafi shall continue to feature in major political discourses throughout Africa and the Middle East; and his life and especially death would every now and then be a source of satisfaction, irritation, controversy, rue, anger and disgust in the rest of the world.

How did this divisive figure who dominated Libyan politics for four decades, who supported Arab and then African unity, who brought significant improvements to the quality of life of Libyans, making them the envy of the rest of Africa, and who was lauded by some for his anti-imperialist stance, ended up isolated, haunted by NATO (North Atlantic Treaty Organization) and finally got killed by Libyans in a civil war where his foreign enemies fought with the Libyan rebels? Why was he strongly opposed by Islamic fundamentalists, condemned by Western powers as a dictator who violated the human rights of his people and financed global terrorism, and why was he kept at arm's length by those he wanted to work with?

We can find some of the answers from the account below.

The controversial Muammar al-Qaddafi who was Africa's long-serving head of state until his ouster and death on October 20, 2011, was born on June 7, 1942, to a tribal family called the al-Qadhafah in the central coastal settlement of Sirte, Libya at a time that Libya was an Italian colony. When in 1951, Libya gained independence as the United Kingdom of Libya, a constitutional and hereditary monarchy under Western-allied King Idris; Qaddafi barely knew what was going on around him. However, the Arab nationalist movement would greatly influence him as a young man, and he would admire its leader, the Egyptian strongman Gamal Abdel Nasser, to the point where he decided to become a soldier like his Egyptian hero, a dream he fulfilled by entering the military college in the eastern Libyan city of Benghazi in 1961. He would eventually spend four months of military training in the United Kingdom.

In Libya, Qaddafi steadily rose through the ranks of the military as the exploitation of oil brought wealth into the country. However, disaffection grew over the increased concentration of the nation's wealth in the hands of King Idris. It was during this time that the talented and charismatic Qaddafi became involved with a movement of young officers bent on overthrowing the king. He would eventually rise to power in the group to the position of leadership. On September 1, 1969, the group overthrew King Idris while he was abroad in Turkey for medical treatment and named Qaddafi the commander in chief of the armed forces and chairman of the Revolutionary Command Council—Libya's new ruling body, effectively making him the ruler of Libya at the age of twenty-seven.

One of the early measures the new authorities took to stamp their authority over the North African country was the immediate shutting down of the American and British military bases in Libya and their forceful demand that foreign oil companies in the country share a bigger proportion of revenue with Libya. That same year, they forbade the sale of alcohol and replaced the Gregorian calendar with the Islamic one.

A failed coup attempt by his fellow officers in December 1969 would make Qaddafi put into place laws criminalizing political dissent. He would go on to expel the remaining Italians from Libya in 1970 and emphasized what he saw as a battle between Arab nationalism and Western imperialism. This would also see him vocally opposing Zionism and Israel, culminating in his expulsion of the Jewish community from the country. As relations with the West soured further and further, Qaddafi's inner circle of trusted people became smaller and smaller, resulting in a police-state whose intelligence agents were audacious enough to even go after Libyans living in exile that they deemed to be working with the enemies of the Libyan state.

The early years of Qaddafi's rule saw him making vigorous attempts to orient Libya away from the West and towards the Middle East and Africa. However, Libya would get into a military conflict with Egypt and Sudan after they tilted towards the West following the signing of the Egyptian-Israeli peace agreement between Nasser's successor Anwar Sadat and the rightwing prime minister of Israel Menachem Begin. Libya would even get involved in the bloody civil war in Chad against the pro-French faction in the conflict.

When in the 1970s Qaddafi published the first volume of the Green Book, which is a three-volume work describing the problems inherent in liberal democracy and capitalism, he raised eyebrows because his opponents saw it as more than an explanation of his political philosophy. In fact, the book was aimed at promoting his policies as the remedy of the outlined problems. His other claims that their New Libya boasted popular committees and shared ownership, generated concerns in several quarters, even though the ideas in the book were not reflected on the ground in Libya the way he claimed.

Even as the lot of the average Libyan under his rule became better to the point of becoming the best in Africa, Qaddafi's foreign enemies were not the only ones who noticed a dose of eccentricity in his style of rule. The fact that he was having a cadre of female bodyguards in heels even though Libya was a Muslim country perched in a region where the issues of women's rights were still in the backwaters; the fact that he considered himself the king of Africa after some African leaders appreciated his drive for an African Union and so awarded him the title; the fact that he was known to erect a tent to stay in when he traveled abroad; the fact that he dressed in outfits that though recognizable in several parts of Africa, did not fit the diplomatic norm; the fact that he was not politically correct and often spoke his mind in a world where most leaders preferred to keep things under the radar; and the fact he would not let Libya become the vassal of any of the big powers, made him a loose cannon in many of the circles of power.

Ronald Reagan, the 40th president of the United States of America would call Qaddafi "The Mad Dog of the Middle East" after concluding that the Libyan leader was not only ruthless in crushing dissent against his autocratic rule at home while his agents hunted down and killed opponents abroad, his government was also implicated in the financing of many anti-Western groups around the world, including groups considered to be terrorist organizations like the Baader Meinhof of Germany, The Japaneses Red Brigade, The Irish Republican Party and the numerous Palestinian groups fighting against Israel. The fact that he was also supporting liberation movements in Africa such as the African National Congress (ANC) in its campaign against Apartheid South Africa, the MPLA against the Portuguese colonial master in Angola, the FRELIMO against Portuguese colonial rule in Mozambique, SWAPO against South African colonial rule in Namibia, and POLISARIO against the Moroccan occupation of Western Sahara; and the fact that he financed coups against African heads of state he considered Western puppets, made him an irritant in the world of "civilized nations".

Following a 1986 bombing of a West Berlin dance club in Germany that killed three and injured scores of people, the United States of America blamed Libya for the terror attack and the US. President Ronald Reagan ordered the bombing of specific targets in Libya, including Qaddafi's residence in Libyan capital city of Tripoli. In the campaign, the United States lost an aircraft that was shot down, resulting in the deaths of two of its crew members. Qaddafi was not killed in the military campaign, but Libya lost 45 soldiers and officials and 15–30 civilians, including a young girl Qaddafi claimed was her adopted daughter called Hanna. In addition, dozens of the North African country's military hardware were destroyed.

Libya was accused of carrying out the 1988 Lockerbie bombing when a plane carrying 259 people blew up near Lockerbie, Scotland, killing all of the passengers onboard. The resulting falling debris would kill an additional 11 civilians on the ground. The United Nations put Libya under sanctions on the grounds that it was implicated in the bombing. But that was not all about it. Several Libyans, including a Qaddafi in-law, were also believed to be behind the explosion of the French passenger jet UTA Flight 772 in 1989, killing all 170 passengers on board the aircraft, including Bonnie Barnes Pugh, the wife of Robert L. Pugh, the United States ambassador to the Republic of Chad, Libya's principal southern neighbor.

There is a school of thought that the rapprochement between Libya and the West that began in the 1990s was from a strong prod from Qaddafi's West-leaning sons. However, the thawing of the relationship between Qaddafi and the West was happening at a time of growing threat from Islamists who opposed his rule. He started sharing information with the British and American intelligence services on containing and neutralizing this growing Islamic fundamentalism.

So, when in 1994, the new president of South Africa Nelson Mandela (he had spent 27 years in Apartheid jail before his release in 1990 that began the peaceful process in the dismantling of Apartheid) persuaded the Libyan leader to hand over the Libyan nationals suspected for plotting the Lockerbie bombing, he acceded. He trusted Nelson Mandela, whom it turned out, was the only foreign leader to visit Libya during the embargo on the country and years of flight ban. The South African statesman's visit marked the beginning of the mending of relations with the West on many fronts, and appeared to many, to herald a new era in Libyan-Western relations. In fact, it was during the 1990s that Gaddafi stopped giving financial, material and human support to the various Pan-Arab and African movements, especially the Palestinian groups. Instead, he focused on getting sanctions on Libya lifted. Some say he gave up on the Palestinians after Yasser Arafat's Palestinian Liberation Organization (PLO) failed to inform him of the secret negotiations they were conducting with the Israelis that eventually led to the signing of the September 13, 1993 Oslo I Accords on reaching a peace deal between Israel and the Palestinians. His pariah status at the time came about mostly from Libya's actions in support of Palestinians.

The September 11, 2001 terrorist attacks in the USA would alter the geostrategic landscape of the world, especially when George W. Bush, the 43rd president of the United States of America stated that "Either you are with us or you are against us." It was whispered in high circles shortly after those attacks that the United States intended to bring down the regimes in the countries George Bush accused of being the "Axis of Evil", comprising Iran, Iraq, North Korea, Cuba, Libya, Sudan and Syria. So, when Libya peacefully resolved with the USA on December 2003 to eliminate its weapons of mass destruction program, including a decades-old nuclear weapons program, many people doubted the Libyan leader's claim that he wanted the program scrapped because he did not want those weapons to fall into the hands of terrorist. They held instead that Qaddafi got rid of his program of weapons of mass destruction because threats from the United States of America that he could not bear, and so succumbed to the demands.

Many Qaddafi critics were not happy that the Libyan leader became welcomed in Western capitals. When the Italian Prime Minister Silvio Berlusconi boasted publicly that he was among Qaddafi's close his friends, many critics of the Libyan strongman wondered whether the newfound friendship of Qaddafi and the West wasn't based on business and access to Libyan oil.

For years, Qaddafi's sons, and more especially his son and heir apparent, Seif al-Islam Qaddafi, mixed freely with London's high society and other high societies in several parts of Europe and America. As if to reward Libya and its strongman for "changing their ways", the United Nations eased sanctions on Libya in 2001, which made it easy for foreign oil companies to work out lucrative new contracts to operate freely in the country. The result was not only a massive injection of capital into Libya, but also an improvement in the living standards, more freedom in the country and greater exposure to the outside world.

When some Arabs accused Qaddafi of giving Israel a stronger strategic edge in the region with the disarmament, of giving credence to U. S. doctrine of preemptive war, and for failing to get security guarantees for Libya and the Arab world, the Libyan government and its supporters responded that giving up its nuclear weapons program enabled Libya to return to the fold of the international community of nations, get a temporary United Nations Security Council seat, and save some money for investing in the Libyan people and in developing the country.

Many Qaddafi supporters, especially in Africa, hold that Qaddafi tapped Libya's economic resurgence into political capital in the continent and started promoting the quick realization of an African Economic Union with a gold-backed currency called the Dinar that would have effectively curtailed France's domineering neocolonialist role in Francophone Africa, thereby making him intolerable in the eyes of France and its Western allies. However, his critics think his dictatorial rule, obstinacy and inability to adjust to the clamor for democracy and freedom sparked off the protest against his rule, a demand for fundamental change of the system that degenerated into an uprising, and then into a civil war.

Qaddafi initially thought the Arab Spring that began in Libya's eastern neighbor Tunisia in January 2011, and then spread to its western neighbor Egypt the next month, resulting in the ouster of Zine El Abidine Ben Ali and Hosni Muburak of Tunisia and Egypt respectively, would bypass Libya. But that was not the case. He had been in power for four decades and could not be insusceptible to opposition. The political changes in Libya's eastern and western neighbors boosted the morale of citizens of the various Arab countries to protest. In Libya, demonstrations broke out in the eastern city of Benghazi, which is Libya's second largest city that is known for its history of opposition to the capital city Tripoli, and then spread throughout Libya, despite the carrot and stick measures undertaken by the Qaddafi regime to abate the situation.

Qaddafi's early indecisive measures emboldened the protesters and the standoff quickly degenerated into an armed uprising. His critics accused him of escalating the situation, for carrying out a bloody repression and for using foreign mercenaries. Qaddafi on his part claimed the demonstrators were traitors, foreigners, al-Qaeda followers and drug addicts. He urged his supporters to continue the fight against the new resistance.

By the end of February 2011, the rebels had formed a governing body called the National Transitional Council in February 2011. At the end of March, a French-led NATO coalition began to provide support for the rebel forces in the form of airstrikes and a no-fly zone, with logistical support provided by the USA. NATO's military intervention over the next six months would destroy the Libyan Air Force and decimate the country's Armed Forces, so that most of those fighting for Qaddafi ended up being people who had no connection with the regular army. NATO's attacks proved to be decisive as one Libyan city after the other fell into rebel hands and as an airstrike killed Qaddafi's youngest son Saif al-Arab Qaddafi, and three of his grandchildren as the Libyan leader and his wife, Safiyahs were attending a gathering of family and friends hosted by their son Said al-Arab.

When in June 2011, the International Criminal Court issued warrants for the arrest of Qaddafi, his son Seif al-Islam, and his brother-in-law for crimes against humanity, the world understood that the powers that be had completed disavowed Qaddafi and that there was no future for his regime. When a month after the indictments, more than 30 countries recognized the NTC as the legitimate government of Libya, it was understood that Qaddafi had lost the civil war.

Tripoli the capital fell to rebel forces in late August 2011, bringing about a symbolic end of Qaddafi's rule as he retreated to Sirte, his hometown, even though most of his enemies could not say for certain where he was. He had basically lost control of Libya, but his whereabouts could not be ascertained.

So, when on October 20, 2011, the world learned that Muammar al-Qaddafi had died near his hometown of Sirte, Libya after a NATO aerial attack on his convoy forced him to hide in a ditch, whence he was discovered by fighters who proceeded to kill him; many people found the news disquieting. However, videos surfaced, showing Qaddafi's bloodied body being dragged around by rebel fighters, then his dead body on display, the last live moments of his other son Mutassim Gaddafi, and later of Mutassim's lifeless body after he had been executed.

While news of Qaddafi's death spread around, spurring many Libyans to pour into the streets in celebration of what many of them hailed as the culmination of their revolution and the start of a new chapter in their history, others saw it as proof that former colonial powers who did not have the interests of the Libyan people at heart had succeeded in defeating a major bulwark to further or continuous foreign exploitation and control of Libya and Africa. This sentiment was deeply felt in the Middle East, and more especially in Africa, where news had reached many that

Qaddafi had stashed away gold and silver valued at more than $7 billion, which he intended for use to establish a pan-African currency based on the Libyan golden Dinar, a currency that would have provided the countries of Francophone African with an alternative currency to the French Franc (CFA).

The media (especially in the Middle Eastern) speculated that the overthrow and killing of Qaddafi would make Iran, North Korea, and possibly other countries, more reluctant to give up their nuclear programs and/or nuclear weapons due to the risk of being weakened and/or double-crossed afterwards. Many in Africa accused the big powers of double-standards, wondering why the Western powers have been rubbing shoulders with dictators like African dictators like Paul Biya of Cameroon (in power since 1982), the Bongos (Omar, from 2 December, 02 1967 – June 08, 2009, and now his son Ali since October 16 2009), the Eyademas (Gnassingbé, from April 14, 1967 – February 5, 2005, and his son Faure Essozimna since May, 04 2005), dictators who impoverished their people, are loathed across the board, and who fragrantly rig elections to stay in power—a sacrilege to democracy that their puppeteers turn a blind eye to or give their blessings to.

As post-Qaddafi Libya continues to be embroiled in violence six years after his death, as armed Islamists make the country ungovernable, as warlords and armed militias abound and create a situation that makes Libya a collection of fiefdoms, as two rival governments reign in the country, many wonder whether Libya would be able to come up any time soon with a functioning system that is better than the rule of the heavily flawed, power-hungry, ruthless but patriotic Muammar Qaddafi who failed to leave behind a peaceful legacy that could be emulated by future generations, a failure that is making it possible for the foreign forces he had ardently wished to keep out of Libya to have a free hand in shaping or failing to shape the country's future.

The ripple effect of the Libyan civil-war spread across North and West Africa, as thousands of combatants, mostly ethnic Tuaregs from Mali and Niger who supported either Gaddafi or the NTC during the conflict, returned to their home countries with a wide range of weapons and ammunition, setting off a trail of civil conflicts in Niger, Mali, Algeria, Nigeria, Cameroon, Chad, and Central African Republic. Today, there is little clamor for an African Economic Union as no other African head of state has stepped forward to lead the effort after the death of Qaddafi, leaving the continent today as the last frontier in a new quest by the industrial powers of the world to secure rapidly dwindling resources.